Contents

Cambridge School
Shakespeare

This edition of *Macbeth* is part of the **Cambridge School Shakespeare** series. Like every other play in the series, it has been specially prepared to help all students in schools and colleges.

This *Macbeth* aims to be different from other editions of the play. It invites you to bring the play to life in your classroom, hall or drama studio through enjoyable activities that will increase your understanding. Actors have created their different interpretations of the play over the centuries. Similarly, you are encouraged to make up your own mind about *Macbeth*, rather than having someone else's interpretation handed down to you.

Cambridge School Shakespeare does not offer you a cut-down or simplified version of the play. This is Shakespeare's language, filled with imaginative possibilities. You will find on every left-hand page: a summary of the action, an explanation of unfamiliar words, a choice of activities on Shakespeare's language, characters and stories.

Between each act and in the pages at the end of the play, you will find notes, illustrations and activities. These will help to increase your understanding of the whole play.

There are a large number of activities to give you the widest choice to suit your own particular needs. Please don't think you have to do every one. Choose the activities that will help you most.

This edition will be of value to you whether you are studying for an examination, reading for pleasure, or thinking of putting on the play to entertain others. You can work on the activities on your own or in groups. Many of the activities suggest a particular group size, but don't be afraid to make up larger or smaller groups to suit your own purposes.

Although you are invited to treat *Macbeth* as a play, you don't need special dramatic or theatrical skills to do the activities. By choosing your activities, and by exploring and experimenting, you can make your own interpretations of Shakespeare's language, characters and stories. Whatever you do, remember that Shakespeare wrote his plays to be acted, watched and enjoyed.

Rex Gibson

This edition of *Macbeth* uses the text of the play established by A. R. Braunmuller in **The New Cambridge Shakespeare**.

Cambridge School
Shakespeare

Macbeth

Edited by Rex Gibson

Series Editor: Rex Gibson
Director, Shakespeare and Schools Project

CAMBRIDGE
UNIVERSITY PRESS

CAMBRIDGE UNIVERSITY PRESS
Cambridge, New York, Melbourne, Madrid, Cape Town,
Singapore, São Paulo, Delhi, Mexico City

Cambridge University Press
The Edinburgh Building, Cambridge CB2 8RU, UK

www.cambridge.org
Information on this title: www.cambridge.org/9780521606868

First published 1993
Second edition 2005
12th printing 2013

Printed and bound in the United Kingdom by the MPG Books Group

A catalogue record for this publication is available from the British Library

ISBN 978-0-521-60686-8 Paperback
ISBN 978-3-12-576237-4 Klett edition

ACKNOWLEDGEMENTS
Thanks are due to the following for permission to reproduce illustrations:
Cover, v, vi, vii, viii, ix, x, xi, xii, 10, 46, 50, 64, 76, 84, 97, 102, 110, 126, 131*b*, 152,
159, 165, 171, 175, 176, 177, 178, Donald Cooper/Photostage; 28, 134, Joe Cocks Stu-
dio Collection © Shakespeare Birthplace Trust; 37*tl*, The Art Archive/Garrick Club;
37*tr*, Alastair Muir; 37*bl*, 148, Columbia Pictures; 63, by permission of the Shakespeare
Birthplace Trust Records Office; 92*l*, 92*r* and 116 Getty Images/Hulton Archive; 104,
by permission of the Shakespeare Birthplace Trust; 131*tl*, by permission of the British
Library (C.27.B.35); 131*tr* Gordon Anthony/Getty Images/Hulton Archive; 132, Morris
Newcombe; 142, from *Gustav Doré: das graphische Werk*, vol. 2, p.1052; 166, Toho/The
Kobal Collection; 179, 'Umbatha: The Zulu Macbeth' at Shakespeare's Globe 1997,
photo John Tramper.

Cover design by Smith

Macbeth dramatises the story of a brave soldier who is tempted by witches and urged by his wife to murder his way to the throne of Scotland. But having killed King Duncan, Macbeth's conscience tortures him and increasingly isolates him from the ambitious Lady Macbeth. You can find other portrayals of the Macbeths in these colour pages and on pages 37, 46, 76, 97, 175, 176 and 177.

The three witches who tempt Macbeth into murder have been portrayed in very different ways on stage. You can find other pictures of witches on pages 10, 102, 131 and 178.

Partners in crime. 'Give me the daggers'. Lady Macbeth wrestles the blood-stained daggers from Macbeth, who is afraid to return them to the room where he has murdered Duncan.

'A little water clears us of this deed'. Lady Macbeth, sharing blood-stained hands with her husband, is unaware that Duncan's murder will come back to haunt her.

The Porter of Macbeth's castle not only provides comic relief but also symbolises major themes of the play. He imagines he is 'porter of hell-gate', reminding the audience of the devilish murder Macbeth has just committed. The Porter's joke about 'an equivocator' (someone who does not tell the whole truth) echoes the theme of deception that runs through the whole play.

For a different portrayal of the Porter see page 50.

What is the relationship of Macbeth and his wife? Although she dominates him in the first two acts, many productions show a loving relationship between them. In the play he calls her 'dearest love', 'dear wife', 'dearest chuck' and 'sweet remembrancer'.

False face. In this Taiwanese adaptation, *The Kingdom of Desire*, Lady Macbeth tries to keep up appearances at the banquet as Macbeth reacts violently to the sight of Banquo's Ghost (Macbeth has had Banquo murdered shortly before the banquet).

'All the perfumes of Arabia will not sweeten this little hand'. Lady Macbeth is tormented by thoughts of all the evil that has followed from her urging Macbeth to seize the crown. In her sleepwalking she remembers how once she had thought that 'a little water' could wash the blood from her and Macbeth's hands. But the bloodstains remain in her mind and have driven her to a mental breakdown.

Portrait of a tyrant. In 2004 the Out of Joint company portrayed Macbeth as Idi Amin Dada, the dictator of Uganda. Amin terrorised his country and was bizarrely obsessed by witchcraft and by Scotland (he even offered himself to Scotland as its king). Amin seized power in 1971, and under his brutal and despotic rule Uganda became like Scotland under Macbeth: 'poor country / Almost afraid to know itself'. He liquidated those he saw as his enemies and became increasingly paranoid and volatile. He was finally overthrown in 1979, but unlike Macbeth Amin went into exile and died peacefully in his bed.

'Hail, King of Scotland'. Macduff has slain Macbeth and now kneels with other thanes to offer homage to Malcolm. Here Macbeth's body lies on stage, but many productions show Macduff bringing in Macbeth's severed head.

'Henceforth be earls'. In the final speech of the play, Malcolm, son of Duncan, grants earldoms to Macduff and the other thanes. Has peace finally been restored to Scotland? (see page 156).

List of characters

The Royal House of Scotland

DUNCAN King of Scotland
MALCOLM his elder son
DONALDBAIN his younger son

Thanes (noblemen of Scotland)
their households and supporters

MACBETH Thane of Glamis
  later Thane of Cawdor
  later King of Scotland
LADY MACBETH
GENTLEWOMAN her attendant
SEYTON Macbeth's armour
  bearer
PORTER at Macbeth's castle
CAPTAIN wounded in battle
AN OLD MAN
DOCTOR of physic
FIRST MURDERER
SECOND MURDERER
THIRD MURDERER

BANQUO
FLEANCE Banquo's son
MACDUFF Thane of Fife
LADY MACDUFF
SON OF MACDUFF

ROSS
LENNOX
MENTEITH } other thanes
ANGUS
CAITHNESS

The supernatural world

THREE WITCHES the weird
  sisters
THREE APPARITIONS

HECATE Queen of Witchcraft
THREE OTHER WITCHES

The English

SIWARD Earl of Northumberland
YOUNG SIWARD his son
ENGLISH DOCTOR at the court of King Edward the Confessor

Lords, Soldiers, Attendants, Servants, Messengers

The play is set in Scotland and England

Three Witches vow to meet Macbeth after the battle. They respond to the calls of their familiar spirits. They leave, chanting ominous words. In Scene 2 Duncan hopes for a battle-report from a wounded Captain.

---

1 Menace and mystery (in groups of three or more)

The best thing to do with Scene 1 is to act it out. It doesn't take long to learn the lines. Present it as dramatically as you can, using sound effects of thunder, rain, battle sounds, a mewing cat and croaking toad (see **2** below). Think about how you can create a menacing and mysterious mood, especially in the final two lines, which ominously reverse values of goodness and beauty. Notice that line 12 reads the same backwards and forwards: 'Fair is foul, and foul is fair'. Use some of the following to help your preparation:

- How do the Witches enter and move?
- Are they old or young? Male or female? (In Shakespeare's time they were played by males.)
- How is each Witch different from the others?
- How are they dressed? What are they carrying? (Have they been scavenging on the battlefield?)
- What actions do they perform as they speak?

After your performance, write notes to guide others how to act out Scene 1.

2 Familiars: Graymalkin and Paddock (in pairs)

Witches were believed to have familiar spirits ('familiars'): demons who helped with their evil work. They usually took the form of animals or birds. In Scene 1 two Witches respond to the cries of their familiars: 'Graymalkin' (a grey cat) and 'Paddock' (a toad). But the Third Witch does not name her familiar; she says only that she'll come at once ('Anon'). Talk together about what creature the Third Witch's familiar might be. Invent a name for it and incorporate the sound it makes into your performance (see **1** above).

---

hurly-burly fighting, confusion
ere before
Graymalkin/Paddock grey cat / toad
  (see **2** above)
Alarum trumpet call to battle

sergeant a soldier who, at the time, could be the equivalent of a captain
hardy brave
fought / 'Gainst my captivity rescued me from capture

Macbeth

Act 1 Scene 1
A desolate place

Thunder and lightning. Enter three WITCHES

FIRST WITCH When shall we three meet again?
In thunder, lightning, or in rain?
SECOND WITCH When the hurly-burly's done,
When the battle's lost, and won.
THIRD WITCH That will be ere the set of sun.   5
FIRST WITCH Where the place?
SECOND WITCH Upon the heath.
THIRD WITCH There to meet with Macbeth.
FIRST WITCH I come, Graymalkin.
SECOND WITCH Paddock calls.   10
THIRD WITCH Anon.
ALL Fair is foul, and foul is fair,
Hover through the fog and filthy air.

Exeunt

Act 1 Scene 2
King Duncan's camp near Forres

Alarum within. Enter King [DUNCAN,] MALCOLM, DONALD-
BAIN, LENNOX, with Attendants, meeting a bleeding CAPTAIN

DUNCAN What bloody man is that? He can report,
As seemeth by his plight, of the revolt
The newest state.
MALCOLM   This is the sergeant
Who like a good and hardy soldier fought
'Gainst my captivity. Hail, brave friend;   5

3

The wounded Captain reports that although the rebel Macdonald had strong forces, Macbeth personally killed him. Facing an assault by fresh Norwegian troops, Macbeth and Banquo fought on undaunted.

---

1 The Captain's story (in groups of four or more)

The Captain's report (lines 7–42) is action-packed. Phrase by phrase, he creates a vivid picture of the battle. One person reads slowly, a small section at a time, pausing after each short phrase. The others mime the action described. For example, the first few sections might be:

'Doubtful it stood' (mime doubt)
'As two spent swimmers' (mime exhaustion)
'that do cling together / And choke their art' (mime drowning)
'The merciless Macdonald' (mime pitiless warrior), and so on.

You will find that this activity helps you to understand how such short units of language pack the Captain's tale with energy and meaning.

2 Words to create atmosphere (in pairs)

One partner reads aloud lines 1–44. The other partner echoes every word to do with war, fighting or armies. Change over and repeat the activity. How many such 'warfare' words can you find? (It will help you to know that 'kerns and galloglasses' are lightly and heavily armed soldiers respectively.) Afterwards, talk together about how Shakespeare creates atmosphere through the vocabulary he uses.

3 The wounded Captain writes home

Imagine you are the wounded Captain. You have had your wounds dressed and now you write home to tell your family what has happened. Base your letter on lines 1–42.

---

broil battle
Fortune fickle luck
Valour's minion bravery's favourite
nave to th'chaps navel to the jaws
'gins his reflection begins to fade
trust their heels run away

surveying vantage seeing an opportunity
furbished polished, cleaned
sooth truth
memorise another Golgotha re-enact a slaughter like Christ's crucifixion

Say to the king, the knowledge of the broil
As thou didst leave it.

CAPTAIN   Doubtful it stood,
As two spent swimmers that do cling together
And choke their art. The merciless Macdonald –
Worthy to be a rebel, for to that   10
The multiplying villainies of nature
Do swarm upon him – from the Western Isles
Of kerns and galloglasses is supplied,
And Fortune on his damnèd quarrel smiling,
Showed like a rebel's whore. But all's too weak,   15
For brave Macbeth – well he deserves that name –
Disdaining Fortune, with his brandished steel,
Which smoked with bloody execution,
Like Valour's minion carved out his passage
Till he faced the slave,   20
Which ne'er shook hands, nor bade farewell to him,
Till he unseamed him from the nave to th'chaps
And fixed his head upon our battlements.

DUNCAN O valiant cousin, worthy gentleman.

CAPTAIN As whence the sun 'gins his reflection,   25
Shipwrecking storms and direful thunders,
So from that spring whence comfort seemed to come,
Discomfort swells. Mark, King of Scotland, mark,
No sooner justice had, with valour armed,
Compelled these skipping kerns to trust their heels,   30
But the Norwegian lord, surveying vantage,
With furbished arms and new supplies of men
Began a fresh assault.

DUNCAN Dismayed not this our captains, Macbeth and Banquo?

CAPTAIN Yes, as sparrows, eagles, or the hare, the lion. 35
If I say sooth, I must report they were
As cannons over-charged with double cracks;
So they doubly redoubled strokes upon the foe.
Except they meant to bathe in reeking wounds
Or memorise another Golgotha,   40
I cannot tell.
But I am faint, my gashes cry for help.

Ross tells that Macbeth has triumphed, capturing Cawdor and obtaining ransom and a favourable peace treaty from the King of Norway. Duncan sentences Cawdor to death and confers his title on Macbeth.

---

1 What is Macbeth like? (in pairs)

In a play, the audience gains its impression of a character from what the character says, what they do, and what other characters say about them. Macbeth has not yet appeared, but in Scene 2 he has been much talked about. From your reading of the scene, pool your thoughts and write down a list of qualities you think Macbeth possesses. As you work through the play add other qualities to your list.

2 Give Angus a voice (in groups of three)

Angus enters but says nothing. Give him the chance to add his own perspective on the story Ross tells. One person reads Duncan, another reads Ross (lines 47–67). Ross pauses after every punctuation mark. In each pause the third person, as Angus, adds their own retelling of Ross's report, explaining each part of it to the king (who might well ask for additional information). For example, after Ross's 'God save the king', Angus might say 'Greetings, your majesty. We salute you'; after 'From Fife', he might add 'In greatest haste', and so on.

3 Show the image (in small groups)

Scene 2 is rich in imagery. Choose one image that particularly appeals to you, for example 'As two spent swimmers', 'multiplying villainies of nature', 'like a rebel's whore', 'as sparrows, eagles', 'another Golgotha'. Prepare a tableau (a 'human sculpture', like a still photograph) of your chosen image. Show your frozen moment to the class, holding still for about thirty seconds. The other groups in the class guess which image you have chosen.

Afterwards, talk together about which you think is the 'easiest' image to portray, and which is the most difficult. Why?

Bellona   Roman goddess of war
bridegroom   (Macbeth)
lapped in proof   clad in armour
self-comparisons   similar actions
Point against point   sword to sword

composition   a peace treaty
deign   permit
Saint Colm's Inch   Isle of Incholm (see map, page 60)
bosom interest   heartfelt concerns
present   immediate

DUNCAN So well thy words become thee as thy wounds;
       They smack of honour both. Go get him surgeons.

                   [Exit Captain, attended]

       Enter ROSS *and* ANGUS

       Who comes here?
MALCOLM   The worthy Thane of Ross.   45
LENNOX What a haste looks through his eyes! So should he look
       That seems to speak things strange.
ROSS   God save the king.
DUNCAN Whence cam'st thou, worthy thane?
ROSS   From Fife, great king,
       Where the Norwegian banners flout the sky
       And fan our people cold.   50
       Norway himself, with terrible numbers,
       Assisted by that most disloyal traitor,
       The Thane of Cawdor, began a dismal conflict,
       Till that Bellona's bridegroom, lapped in proof,
       Confronted him with self-comparisons,   55
       Point against point, rebellious arm 'gainst arm,
       Curbing his lavish spirit. And to conclude,
       The victory fell on us –
DUNCAN   Great happiness! –
ROSS   That now Sweno,
       The Norways' king, craves composition.
       Nor would we deign him burial of his men   60
       Till he disbursèd at Saint Colm's Inch
       Ten thousand dollars to our general use.
DUNCAN No more that Thane of Cawdor shall deceive
       Our bosom interest. Go pronounce his present death
       And with his former title greet Macbeth.   65
ROSS I'll see it done.
DUNCAN What he hath lost, noble Macbeth hath won.

                   Exeunt

The Witches await Macbeth. They plot to torment a sea-captain whose wife has insulted them. A drum signals the approach of Macbeth.

---

1 Speak the Witches' language! (in groups of three)

The Witches have a style of speaking all of their own. To gain the feel of their language, take parts and read aloud all they say between lines 1 and 67 (ignore what Macbeth and Banquo say). As you read, add actions that you feel are suitable. After your reading, talk together about the way the Witches speak, and why you think Shakespeare gives them that particular style of speech. How many words can you find to describe it? (A hint: don't be afraid to use a thesaurus to find appropriate words.)

2 The master of the *Tiger*

a In 1606 (the year in which *Macbeth* was probably written) an English ship called the *Tiger* did in fact limp home after a disaster-struck voyage of 567 days ($7 \times 9 \times 9$, see line 21). Imagine you are the ship-captain and write an account of your perilous sea journey. Use your imagination, just as Shakespeare did. He was more concerned with the dramatic and imaginative possibilities of the stories he heard and read than with their factual accuracy (the storm-battered *Tiger* actually sailed to Japan, and Aleppo is sixty miles inland from the Mediterranean coast).

b The Witch's story seems to have little to do with the play. Or does it? Suggest one or two possible reasons why Shakespeare wrote lines 1–27.

3 'Aroint thee, witch'

Line 5 is the only time in the play when the word 'witch' is used. See pages vi, 10, 131 and 178 for examples of how the three weird sisters do not have to appear as conventional witches.

---

quoth said	**card** compass
Aroint thee clear off	**penthouse lid** eyelid
rump-fed runnion pampered slut	**forbid** cursed
very ports they blow winds prevent ships from entering every port	**sennights** seven nights
	bark ship
quarters directions	**pilot** guide who steers ships to harbour

Act 1 Scene 3
A heath

Thunder. Enter the three WITCHES

FIRST WITCH Where hast thou been, sister?

SECOND WITCH Killing swine.

THIRD WITCH   Sister, where thou?

FIRST WITCH A sailor's wife had chestnuts in her lap
    And munched, and munched, and munched. 'Give me',
        quoth I.
    'Aroint thee, witch', the rump-fed runnion cries.   5
    Her husband's to Aleppo gone, master o'th'Tiger:
    But in a sieve I'll thither sail,
    And like a rat without a tail,
    I'll do, I'll do, and I'll do.

SECOND WITCH I'll give thee a wind.   10

FIRST WITCH Thou'rt kind.

THIRD WITCH And I another.

FIRST WITCH I myself have all the other,
    And the very ports they blow,
    All the quarters that they know   15
    I'th'shipman's card.
    I'll drain him dry as hay:
    Sleep shall neither night nor day
    Hang upon his penthouse lid;
    He shall live a man forbid.   20
    Weary sennights nine times nine,
    Shall he dwindle, peak, and pine.
    Though his bark cannot be lost,
    Yet it shall be tempest-tossed.
    Look what I have.

SECOND WITCH   Show me, show me.   25

FIRST WITCH Here I have a pilot's thumb,
    Wrecked as homeward he did come.
        Drum within

THIRD WITCH A drum, a drum;
    Macbeth doth come.

The Witches chant a spell to prepare for their meeting with Macbeth. They amaze him with predictions that he will be Thane of Cawdor and King of Scotland. Banquo demands to know his own future.

'Speak if you can', Macbeth demands. Speak the Witches' predictions in lines 46–8 as you think they would deliver them (think about tone of voice, gesture and movement).

1 'So foul and fair a day' (in pairs)

Macbeth's first words echo the Witches' last lines in Act 1 Scene 1. Talk together about whether you think they suggest that conflict and insecurity exist in his mind, even though he has just won a great battle.

weïrd sisters   (in Anglo-Saxon mythology) goddesses of destiny who predicted the future (see page 36)
Posters   fast travellers
charm   spell
Forres   see map, page 60

aught   anything
Glamis   (pronounced 'Glahms' – that is, one syllable)
fantastical   imaginary
noble having   new titles of nobility
rapt   spellbound
seeds of time   future

ALL   The weïrd sisters, hand in hand,   30
      Posters of the sea and land,
      Thus do go, about, about,
      Thrice to thine, and thrice to mine,
      And thrice again, to make up nine.
      Peace, the charm's wound up.   35

Enter MACBETH *and* BANQUO

MACBETH   So foul and fair a day I have not seen.
BANQUO   How far is't called to Forres? What are these,
      So withered and so wild in their attire,
      That look not like th'inhabitants o'th'earth,
      And yet are on't? – Live you, or are you aught   40
      That man may question? You seem to understand me,
      By each at once her choppy finger laying
      Upon her skinny lips; you should be women,
      And yet your beards forbid me to interpret
      That you are so.
MACBETH   Speak if you can: what are you?   45
FIRST WITCH   All hail Macbeth, hail to thee, Thane of Glamis.
SECOND WITCH   All hail Macbeth, hail to thee, Thane of Cawdor.
THIRD WITCH   All hail Macbeth, that shalt be king hereafter.
BANQUO   Good sir, why do you start and seem to fear
      Things that do sound so fair? – I'th'name of truth   50
      Are ye fantastical, or that indeed
      Which outwardly ye show? My noble partner
      You greet with present grace and great prediction
      Of noble having and of royal hope
      That he seems rapt withal. To me you speak not.   55
      If you can look into the seeds of time
      And say which grain will grow and which will not,
      Speak then to me, who neither beg nor fear
      Your favours nor your hate.
FIRST WITCH   Hail.   60
SECOND WITCH   Hail.
THIRD WITCH   Hail.

The Witches prophesy that Banquo's descendants will be kings, but he himself will not. Refusing to answer Macbeth's questions, the Witches vanish. Ross brings news of Duncan's delight at Macbeth's victory.

1 How do the Witches vanish? (in pairs)

Every director of the play has to solve the practical puzzle of the stage direction '*Witches vanish*'. How can you convincingly get them off stage, vanishing before the audience's eyes? Work out your suggestions for making the Witches vanish in a production set somewhere in your school or college.

2 Three types of language? (in groups of three)

Here is a director of the play giving advice to actors in rehearsal:

- In lines 68–76 Macbeth just can't believe what he has heard. He wants answers, urgently. So speak the lines fast and angrily.
- In lines 77–86 the two men are deeply puzzled and amazed by what they have seen and heard. So speak the lines slowly and wonderingly.
- In lines 87–98 Ross wants to impress Macbeth and Banquo with the importance of his news and his own importance. So speak the lines pompously and grandly.

Take parts and carry out the director's suggestions. Then talk together about whether you think the advice is appropriate. Write your own suggestions for how the lines could be spoken to greatest dramatic effect.

3 'Strange images of death' (in groups of six or more)

Ross praises Macbeth. He reports that when fighting the Norwegians, Macbeth made 'Strange images of death' (line 95). Work out a tableau of one of these strange images. Some of the wounded Captain's report from Scene 2 might help you to construct your image.

---

get be father of
Finel Macbeth's father (see page 62)
Stands not . . . belief is
 unbelievable
intelligence knowledge
corporal physical

the insane root hemlock, henbane or
 deadly nightshade (when eaten, it
 produces madness)
Nothing afeard not afraid
tale hail(?)
post with post many messages

FIRST WITCH Lesser than Macbeth, and greater.

SECOND WITCH Not so happy, yet much happier.

THIRD WITCH Thou shalt get kings, though thou be none.   65
      So all hail Macbeth and Banquo.

FIRST WITCH Banquo and Macbeth, all hail.

MACBETH Stay, you imperfect speakers. Tell me more.
      By Finel's death, I know I am Thane of Glamis,
      But how of Cawdor? The Thane of Cawdor lives   70
      A prosperous gentleman, and to be king
      Stands not within the prospect of belief,
      No more than to be Cawdor. Say from whence
      You owe this strange intelligence, or why
      Upon this blasted heath you stop our way   75
      With such prophetic greeting? Speak, I charge you.

Witches vanish

BANQUO The earth hath bubbles, as the water has,
      And these are of them. Whither are they vanished?

MACBETH Into the air, and what seemed corporal,
      Melted, as breath into the wind. Would they had stayed.   80

BANQUO Were such things here as we do speak about?
      Or have we eaten on the insane root,
      That takes the reason prisoner?

MACBETH Your children shall be kings.

BANQUO   You shall be king.

MACBETH And Thane of Cawdor too: went it not so?   85

BANQUO To th'selfsame tune and words – who's here?

Enter ROSS *and* ANGUS

ROSS The king hath happily received, Macbeth,
      The news of thy success, and when he reads
      Thy personal venture in the rebels' sight,
      His wonders and his praises do contend   90
      Which should be thine or his. Silenced with that,
      In viewing o'er the rest o'th'selfsame day,
      He finds thee in the stout Norwegian ranks,
      Nothing afeard of what thyself didst make,
      Strange images of death. As thick as tale   95
      Came post with post, and every one did bear
      Thy praises in his kingdom's great defence,
      And poured them down before him.

Macbeth is amazed to hear that he is now Thane of Cawdor. Angus explains that the treacherous thane has been sentenced to death. Banquo warns that the Witches' predictions might lead to evil.

1 Notice of execution

Angus tells that the present Thane of Cawdor is alive but has committed treachery of some kind. Use lines 107–115 to help you write the official notice which gives reasons for Cawdor's conviction for treason and announces his imminent execution.

2 'Why do you dress me / In borrowed robes?'

Lines 106–7 provide the first of many images of clothing in the play. As you read through the play look out for other references to clothing and think about how they add to the play's imaginative impact. For example, there is a subtle 'clothes' reference in line 111, where 'line' also means the lining or reinforcement of a cloak (Cawdor had reinforced the rebel Macdonald's forces).

3 'The greatest is behind' (in pairs)

Line 116 suggests that Macbeth is beginning to think about becoming king ('The greatest'). Talk together about how Macbeth might speak those four words and how his facial expression and gestures might also reveal his thoughts.

4 Macbeth and Banquo (in pairs)

Macbeth and Banquo are comrades in arms who have just won a great victory. But how have the Witches' prophecies affected their relationship? Write notes on how the two men relate to each other during each speech on the opposite page. Are there signs of a growing suspicion of each other?

---

earnest promise
addition new title
heavy judgement sentence of death
line reinforce
trusted home believed fully
enkindle . . . crown fire your desire to become king

instruments of darkness devils (the Witches)
Win us . . . consequence tell us truths about small matters, but lie about great ones
Cousins kinsmen

ANGUS   We are sent
          To give thee from our royal master thanks;
          Only to herald thee into his sight,   100
          Not pay thee.
ROSS And for an earnest of a greater honour,
          He bade me, from him, call thee Thane of Cawdor:
          In which addition, hail most worthy thane,
          For it is thine.
BANQUO   What, can the devil speak true?   105
MACBETH The Thane of Cawdor lives. Why do you dress me
          In borrowed robes?
ANGUS   Who was the thane, lives yet,
          But under heavy judgement bears that life
          Which he deserves to lose.
          Whether he was combined with those of Norway,   110
          Or did line the rebel with hidden help
          And vantage, or that with both he laboured
          In his country's wrack, I know not,
          But treasons capital, confessed and proved,
          Have overthrown him.
MACBETH [*Aside*]   Glamis, and Thane of Cawdor: 115
          The greatest is behind. – Thanks for your pains. –
          [*To Banquo*] Do you not hope your children shall be kings,
          When those that gave the Thane of Cawdor to me
          Promised no less to them?
BANQUO   That trusted home,
          Might yet enkindle you unto the crown,   120
          Besides the Thane of Cawdor. But 'tis strange,
          And oftentimes, to win us to our harm,
          The instruments of darkness tell us truths;
          Win us with honest trifles, to betray's
          In deepest consequence. –   125
          Cousins, a word, I pray you.

Macbeth weighs the moral implications of the Witches' prediction. He is horrified at the thought of killing Duncan, but resolves to accept whatever has to be. He proposes that he and Banquo talk together later.

1 Macbeth's private thoughts (in pairs)

a Macbeth's soliloquy (lines 126–41) reveals his troubled mind. To discover the seesawing movements of his thoughts, link hands with your partner and gently pull or push as you speak the lines to each other. Afterwards, identify the three major antitheses (see pages 171–2) in the lines (the first is 'ill' versus 'good').

b One person reads everything Macbeth says on the opposite page, pausing at the end of each sentence. The other person says 'Hail, King of Scotland' after each sentence. Afterwards, talk together about whether you think that prediction is uppermost in Macbeth's mind each time he speaks.

2 Thoughts of murder? (in groups of three)

At six points in his soliloquy Macbeth uses expressions that could be thoughts of himself murdering Duncan: 'suggestion' (line 133), 'horrid image' (line 134), 'horrible imaginings' (line 137), 'My thought' (line 138), 'surmise' (line 140), 'what is not' (line 141). As one person speaks lines 129–41 the other two, at the appropriate points, mime different versions of the murder.

3 Imagery (in pairs)

Banquo's explanation (lines 141–5) of why Macbeth is spellbound ('rapt') uses the imagery of clothes: new titles like new clothes ('strange garments'), take time to become familiar. Macbeth begins his soliloquy (lines 126–41) with theatrical imagery: 'happy prologues', 'swelling act', 'imperial theme'. Work out what Macbeth means by each of these three images.

---

soliciting promising of pleasure
Present fears . . . imaginings real dangers are less frightening than what I can imagine
function / Is smothered in surmise my imaginings stop me from taking action

Time . . . roughest day what will be, will be
wrought disturbed
things forgotten (Is Macbeth lying?)
The interim having weighed it after time for thought

MACBETH [*Aside*]   Two truths are told,
          As happy prologues to the swelling act
          Of the imperial theme. – I thank you, gentlemen. –
          This supernatural soliciting
          Cannot be ill, cannot be good. If ill,   130
          Why hath it given me earnest of success,
          Commencing in a truth? I am Thane of Cawdor.
          If good, why do I yield to that suggestion,
          Whose horrid image doth unfix my hair
          And make my seated heart knock at my ribs   135
          Against the use of nature? Present fears
          Are less than horrible imaginings.
          My thought, whose murder yet is but fantastical,
          Shakes so my single state of man that function
          Is smothered in surmise, and nothing is,   140
          But what is not.
BANQUO   Look how our partner's rapt.
MACBETH If chance will have me king, why chance may crown me
          Without my stir.
BANQUO   New honours come upon him
          Like our strange garments, cleave not to their mould,
          But with the aid of use.
MACBETH   Come what come may,   145
          Time and the hour runs through the roughest day.
BANQUO Worthy Macbeth, we stay upon your leisure.
MACBETH Give me your favour. My dull brain was wrought
          With things forgotten. Kind gentlemen, your pains
          Are registered where every day I turn   150
          The leaf to read them. Let us toward the king.
          [*To Banquo*] Think upon what hath chanced and at more
              time,
          The interim having weighed it, let us speak
          Our free hearts each to other.
BANQUO   Very gladly.
MACBETH Till then, enough. – Come, friends.   155
                                                      Exeunt

17

Malcolm reports that the Thane of Cawdor died a repentant and dignified death. Duncan reflects that it is impossible to judge anyone by their outward appearance. He warmly welcomes Macbeth.

---

1 Honourable and fearless (in groups of four or more)

The way in which the Thane of Cawdor died was apparently the noblest thing he did in his life: 'Nothing in his life / Became him like the leaving it.' His death is hardly ever shown on stage (but is shown in the film version directed by Roman Polanski). Prepare a presentation to show how Cawdor behaved at his execution. One person narrates lines 5–11 as you stage your scene.

2 Appearances are deceptive (whole class)

You can't tell what people are like from their looks, muses Duncan ('There's no art / To find the mind's construction in the face'). Do you agree? Organise a class debate on Duncan's lines 11–12. You might find it helpful to collect photographs from newspapers (for example, of convicted criminals) to use as evidence for your views.

3 Dramatic irony (in pairs)

Dramatic irony occurs when the audience knows something that the characters in the play do not. Duncan's words about Cawdor ('He was a gentleman on whom I built / An absolute trust') and Macbeth's immediate entry is an example of dramatic irony. As Duncan speaks of 'absolute trust', the man who is thinking about murdering him enters. Talk together about how you think Macbeth should enter to increase the audience's sense of dramatic irony, and then note down your ideas. (For example, in one production the entry of Macbeth seemed unexpected, and caused alarm. Before Macbeth was recognised, Duncan's supporters drew their swords and formed a protective circle around the king.)

Flourish fanfare of trumpets
in commission responsible
Became dignified
studied rehearsed (a theatrical image)
before beyond my power to pay you

recompense suitable reward
That the proportion . . . mine that I could honour you appropriately
More is thy due . . . pay you deserve more than anyone can pay

Act 1 Scene 4
Duncan's palace at Forres

Flourish. Enter King DUNCAN, LENNOX, MALCOLM,
DONALDBAIN, *and Attendants*

DUNCAN Is execution done on Cawdor, or not
    Those in commission yet returned?
MALCOLM   My liege,
    They are not yet come back. But I have spoke
    With one that saw him die, who did report
    That very frankly he confessed his treasons,   5
    Implored your highness' pardon, and set forth
    A deep repentance. Nothing in his life
    Became him like the leaving it. He died
    As one that had been studied in his death,
    To throw away the dearest thing he owed   10
    As 'twere a careless trifle.
DUNCAN   There's no art
    To find the mind's construction in the face.
    He was a gentleman on whom I built
    An absolute trust.

Enter MACBETH, BANQUO, ROSS, *and* ANGUS

                  O worthiest cousin,
    The sin of my ingratitude even now   15
    Was heavy on me. Thou art so far before,
    That swiftest wing of recompense is slow
    To overtake thee. Would thou hadst less deserved,
    That the proportion both of thanks and payment
    Might have been mine. Only I have left to say,   20
    More is thy due than more than all can pay.
MACBETH The service and the loyalty I owe,
    In doing it, pays itself. Your highness' part

Macbeth declares his loyalty to Duncan, who (after promising honours to Macbeth and Banquo) announces that his son, Malcolm, shall succeed to the throne. Macbeth is appalled and broods ominously.

1 Public compliments and private thoughts (in pairs)

Macbeth's six lines to Duncan (lines 22–7) and his six lines to himself (lines 48–53) are strongly contrasted in both meaning and language style. For example, the second speech is almost entirely composed of monosyllabic words.

Take turns to speak lines 22–7. Smile and bow every time you use a word about loyalty or kingship. Then speak lines 48–53 and snarl and make a stabbing gesture every time you speak words that suggest Macbeth's evil intentions. Remember that because of the Witches' prophecy, he has been bitterly disappointed at Duncan's nomination of Malcolm as king.

Afterwards, write your recommendations for how each speech might be spoken on stage to maximise dramatic effect.

2 What is Duncan like? (in pairs)

Most productions present Duncan as a gentle, ideal king. For example, in this scene his words about Cawdor's treachery are full of personal regret, and his language is full of gratitude for the service Macbeth and Banquo have performed. He promises them generous rewards, embraces Banquo, and weeps for joy at their loyalty. His language uses images of growth and of banqueting.

But his action in naming Malcolm as his successor has sometimes been interpreted as suggesting that Duncan is devious. It is a sign he wishes to establish his own dynasty rather than follow the established custom by which a small group of noble kinsmen elected the king.

Talk together about how you would present Duncan on stage. Would he be evidently sincere and noble? Or . . . ?

Wanton unrestrained
We will establish our estate upon I declare as Scotland's next king
invest endow, clothe
Inverness Macbeth's castle
harbinger messenger (an officer who prepared for a king's visit)

The eye wink at the hand don't see the fatal blow
full so supremely
commendations praises or recommendations
peerless matchless

        Is to receive our duties, and our duties
        Are to your throne and state, children and servants,   25
        Which do but what they should by doing everything
        Safe toward your love and honour.
DUNCAN   Welcome hither.
        I have begun to plant thee and will labour
        To make thee full of growing. Noble Banquo,
        That hast no less deserved, nor must be known   30
        No less to have done so, let me enfold thee
        And hold thee to my heart.
BANQUO   There if I grow,
        The harvest is your own.
DUNCAN   My plenteous joys,
        Wanton in fullness, seek to hide themselves
        In drops of sorrow. Sons, kinsmen, thanes,   35
        And you whose places are the nearest, know:
        We will establish our estate upon
        Our eldest, Malcolm, whom we name hereafter
        The Prince of Cumberland, which honour must
        Not unaccompanied invest him only,   40
        But signs of nobleness like stars shall shine
        On all deservers. [*To Macbeth*] From hence to Inverness
        And bind us further to you.
MACBETH The rest is labour which is not used for you;
        I'll be myself the harbinger and make joyful   45
        The hearing of my wife with your approach.
        So humbly take my leave.
DUNCAN   My worthy Cawdor.
MACBETH [*Aside*] The Prince of Cumberland: that is a step
        On which I must fall down, or else o'erleap,
        For in my way it lies. Stars, hide your fires,   50
        Let not light see my black and deep desires,
        The eye wink at the hand. Yet let that be,
        Which the eye fears when it is done to see.   *Exit*
DUNCAN True, worthy Banquo, he is full so valiant,
        And in his commendations I am fed;   55
        It is a banquet to me. Let's after him,
        Whose care is gone before to bid us welcome:
        It is a peerless kinsman.
               Flourish
                         Exeunt

Lady Macbeth reads her husband's letter telling of the Witches' prophecy of kingship. She analyses his nature, fearing that he is too decent and squeamish to murder Duncan for the crown.

---

1 What else did Macbeth write?

Lines 1–12 may be only part of Macbeth's letter to his wife. It concerns only the Witches. What other news did he report? Write the missing parts of the letter, giving details of the battle, his thoughts about Banquo, and his reaction to Duncan having declared Malcolm the next king.

2 A wife's view of her husband (in pairs)

Lady Macbeth analyses her husband's nature. In lines 15–23 she describes at least eight elements of his character. Use the lines to write a list of Macbeth's characteristics as his wife sees them. (To help you: lines 22–3 are very densely expressed; they mean 'what you fear, you don't wish to do'.)

3 Breakfast with the Macbeths (in pairs)

How has Lady Macbeth come to hold this view of her husband? Use the list you have compiled in 2 above to improvise a breakfast-time conversation between the Macbeths. In that conversation, Lady Macbeth gives actual examples of her husband's past behaviour to support her view. (Notice that in lines 24–5 Lady Macbeth gives a clue to her style of speaking to him.)

4 First impressions

This is Lady Macbeth's first appearance. Write some notes on how you visualise her appearance (age, costume, physical appearance).

You will also probably have some initial thoughts about her personality. Note them down. You can add to your list as you read on.

---

in the day of success   on the day of victory in battle
missives   messengers
the coming on of time   the future
What thou art promised   king
catch the nearest way   act without pity

illness   evil
holily   fairly, without evil
Hie   hurry
chastise   punish and remove
golden round   crown
metaphysical   supernatural
tidings   news

Act 1 Scene 5
Macbeth's castle at Inverness

Enter LADY MACBETH *alone, with a letter*

LADY MACBETH [*Reads*] 'They met me in the day of success, and
I have learned by the perfectest report they have more in
them than mortal knowledge. When I burned in desire to
question them further, they made themselves air, into which
they vanished. Whiles I stood rapt in the wonder of it, came   5
missives from the king who all-hailed me Thane of Cawdor, by
which title before these weïrd sisters saluted me and referred
me to the coming on of time, with "Hail, king that shalt be."
This have I thought good to deliver thee, my dearest partner of
greatness, that thou mightst not lose the dues of rejoicing by   10
being ignorant of what greatness is promised thee. Lay it to thy
heart and farewell.'
    Glamis thou art, and Cawdor, and shalt be
    What thou art promised; yet do I fear thy nature,
    It is too full o'th'milk of human kindness   15
    To catch the nearest way. Thou wouldst be great,
    Art not without ambition, but without
    The illness should attend it. What thou wouldst highly,
    That wouldst thou holily; wouldst not play false,
    And yet wouldst wrongly win. Thou'dst have, great
        Glamis,   20
    That which cries, 'Thus thou must do' if thou have it;
    And that which rather thou dost fear to do,
    Than wishest should be undone. Hie thee hither,
    That I may pour my spirits in thine ear
    And chastise with the valour of my tongue   25
    All that impedes thee from the golden round,
    Which fate and metaphysical aid doth seem
    To have thee crowned withal.

Enter [ATTENDANT]

                What is your tidings?
ATTENDANT The king comes here tonight.

The Attendant gives news that Macbeth is approaching. Lady Macbeth calls on evil spirits to assist her plans for Duncan's murder. She greets Macbeth with thoughts of future greatness.

---

1 The language of spells (in groups of four)

Speak Lady Macbeth's lines 36–52 as a spell, calling on evil spirits for assistance. Share the lines between you and experiment with different ways of saying them: whisper them; hiss them fiercely; speak them as if in a trance. Add background sound effects to increase the dramatic intensity of your presentation. Some points to help you:

- The raven was considered to be a bird of ill-omen, associated with death.
- Notice the urgency of the repeated orders: 'Come, you spirits . . .', 'Come to my woman's breasts . . .', 'Come, thick night . . .'.
- The phrase 'make thick my blood' suggests that this will prevent pity reaching her heart.

After your experiments, write about how you think Lady Macbeth could deliver her lines on stage to suggest that she wishes to be utterly free of compassion or gentle feelings.

2 Husband and wife reunite (in pairs)

Lady Macbeth greets her husband with an echo of the Witches' language: 'Great Glamis, worthy Cawdor, / Greater than both by the all-hail hereafter'. But his first words are 'My dearest love'. Suggest what actions might accompany both greetings to show their relationship.

3 Evil intent?

All actors give much thought to how lines 57–8 should be spoken: 'And when goes hence?' / 'Tomorrow, as he purposes.' Are they spoken innocently, or with murder in mind?

---

had the speed of overtook
tending attention, accommodation
unsex me remove my gentler feelings
compunctious compassionate
fell deadly

gall bitter poison
pall wrap (as in a funeral pall or cloak)
dunnest darkest
all-hail hereafter future kingship
in the instant now

LADY MACBETH   Thou'rt mad to say it.
    Is not thy master with him? Who, were't so,   30
    Would have informed for preparation.
ATTENDANT So please you, it is true: our thane is coming.
    One of my fellows had the speed of him;
    Who almost dead for breath, had scarcely more
    Than would make up his message.
LADY MACBETH   Give him tending,   35
    He brings great news.

                            Exit [*Attendant*]

               The raven himself is hoarse
    That croaks the fatal entrance of Duncan
    Under my battlements. Come, you spirits
    That tend on mortal thoughts, unsex me here
    And fill me from the crown to the toe topfull   40
    Of direst cruelty; make thick my blood,
    Stop up th'access and passage to remorse
    That no compunctious visitings of nature
    Shake my fell purpose nor keep peace between
    Th'effect and it. Come to my woman's breasts   45
    And take my milk for gall, you murd'ring ministers,
    Wherever in your sightless substances
    You wait on nature's mischief. Come, thick night,
    And pall thee in the dunnest smoke of hell,
    That my keen knife see not the wound it makes,   50
    Nor heaven peep through the blanket of the dark,
    To cry, 'Hold, hold.'

        Enter MACBETH

              Great Glamis, worthy Cawdor,
    Greater than both by the all-hail hereafter,
    Thy letters have transported me beyond
    This ignorant present, and I feel now   55
    The future in the instant.
MACBETH   My dearest love,
    Duncan comes here tonight.
LADY MACBETH   And when goes hence?
MACBETH Tomorrow, as he purposes.

Lady Macbeth urges Macbeth to hide his deadly intentions behind welcoming looks. She will manage the killing of Duncan. Banquo and Duncan comment on the benign appearance of Macbeth's castle.

---

1 Double meanings

Lady Macbeth's lines 64–8 are filled with double meaning: 'provided for' = fed (or killed); 'business' = feasting (or murder); 'dispatch' = carrying out the welcome (or killing). Does Lady Macbeth use these veiled words because she is:

- testing Macbeth – how will he react to the possibility of murder?
- still unsure herself about the awfulness of murder?
- afraid that direct language will make Macbeth refuse to act?

Consider each possibility in turn, then suggest other probable explanations.

2 Don't trust appearances: dramatic irony (in pairs)

Lines 1–10 are full of praise for the appearance of Macbeth's castle. Duncan admires its position ('seat') and healthy air. Banquo develops an elaborate metaphor as he describes nests of house martins ('loved mansionry') under every convenient ledge ('jutty, frieze, Buttress, . . . coign of vantage'). He voices the belief that martins choose healthy situations to raise their young ('pendent bed', 'procreant cradle'). But in Shakespeare's time 'martlet' (or martin) could mean someone deceived by appearances, a 'dope' or 'dupe'.

Work out how to stage the opening ten lines of Scene 6 to bring out the dramatic irony of Duncan's and Banquo's praise of the benign appearance of Macbeth's castle. Remember the audience have just heard Lady Macbeth planning Duncan's murder with the words 'look like th'innocent flower, / But be the serpent under't' (look friendly, but act treacherously).

---

beguile deceive
sovereign sway kingship
look up clear look innocent
To alter . . . fear a guilty face (favour) reveals itself (or fear results in a guilty face)

Hautboys oboes
seat position, location
martlet martin (see **2** above)
approve prove
pendent hanging

LADY MACBETH   O never
            Shall sun that morrow see.
            Your face, my thane, is as a book where men   60
            May read strange matters. To beguile the time,
            Look like the time, bear welcome in your eye,
            Your hand, your tongue; look like th'innocent flower,
            But be the serpent under't. He that's coming
            Must be provided for, and you shall put   65
            This night's great business into my dispatch,
            Which shall to all our nights and days to come
            Give solely sovereign sway and masterdom.
MACBETH We will speak further –
LADY MACBETH   Only look up clear;
            To alter favour ever is to fear.   70
            Leave all the rest to me.

                                                      Exeunt

Act 1 Scene 6
Outside Macbeth's castle

     Hautboys, and torches. Enter King DUNCAN, MALCOLM,
  DONALDBAIN, BANQUO, LENNOX, MACDUFF, ROSS, ANGUS,
                      and attendants

DUNCAN This castle hath a pleasant seat; the air
            Nimbly and sweetly recommends itself
            Unto our gentle senses.
BANQUO   This guest of summer,
            The temple-haunting martlet, does approve
            By his loved mansionry that the heaven's breath   5
            Smells wooingly here. No jutty, frieze,
            Buttress, nor coign of vantage but this bird
            Hath made his pendent bed and procreant cradle;
            Where they most breed and haunt, I have observed
            The air is delicate.   10

Lady Macbeth welcomes Duncan with elaborately courteous language. She speaks of loyalty, obedience and gratefulness for past honours.

---

1 Ceremony hides Lady Macbeth's insincerity (in pairs)

Duncan and Lady Macbeth exchange many compliments and much flattery. Duncan's lines 11–15 are elaborately courteous and convoluted. He says that love sometimes causes him trouble, but he is grateful for such love. This should teach Lady Macbeth to ask God to reward Duncan for the trouble he is causing her!

Lady Macbeth's flattery, however, hides a sinister purpose. Speak all she says in lines 15–29, but every time she says something insincere, bare your teeth menacingly, then smile (or say 'fair is foul').

Experiment with other ways of showing her hypocrisy. (Remember she is taking her own advice: 'look like th'innocent flower, / But be the serpent under't'.)

Identify who's who, and suggest which line is being spoken here.

God yield us   God reward me
single   weak
contend   balance, weigh
those of old   past honours
late dignities   recent honours
We rest your hermits   we will pray for you constantly

coursed   chased, hunted
purveyor   officer riding ahead to prepare food
in count   in trust (or totally)
make their audit   show their accounts (or give to you)
Still   always

Enter LADY [MACBETH]

DUNCAN   See, see, our honoured hostess. – The love
            That follows us sometime is our trouble,
            Which still we thank as love. Herein I teach you
            How you shall bid God yield us for your pains
            And thank us for your trouble.
LADY MACBETH   All our service,   15
            In every point twice done and then done double,
            Were poor and single business to contend
            Against those honours deep and broad wherewith
            Your majesty loads our house. For those of old,
            And the late dignities heaped up to them,   20
            We rest your hermits.
DUNCAN   Where's the Thane of Cawdor?
            We coursed him at the heels and had a purpose
            To be his purveyor, but he rides well,
            And his great love, sharp as his spur, hath holp him
            To his home before us. Fair and noble hostess, 25
            We are your guest tonight.
LADY MACBETH   Your servants ever
            Have theirs, themselves, and what is theirs in count
            To make their audit at your highness' pleasure,
            Still to return your own.
DUNCAN   Give me your hand;
            Conduct me to mine host: we love him highly   30
            And shall continue our graces towards him.
            By your leave, hostess.
                                        Exeunt

Macbeth struggles with his conscience: killing Duncan will result in vengeance; there are compelling reasons against the murder. Heaven itself will abhor the deed. Only ambition spurs him on.

---

1 To kill or not to kill? (in small groups)

Macbeth agonises over killing Duncan. Experiment with ways of speaking his soliloquy to bring out his uneasy feelings. For example, you could share the lines between you and whisper them, with heads close together, as a tortured conversation. Using the following analysis of the soliloquy, write notes suggesting how an actor might deliver each section on stage:

Lines 1–7   If there were no consequences resulting from the murder, I'd risk it, not worrying about the future.

Lines 7–25 The arguments against killing Duncan:

         8–12 vengeance – the killer will be killed

         13–14 kinship – you don't kill your relatives

         13–14 loyalty – you don't kill your king

         14–16 hospitality – a host doesn't kill his guest

         16–20 Duncan's goodness – you don't kill a virtuous king

         20 (and 7) religion – the killer is damned for eternity

         21–5 pity and horror – murder is unnatural to innocent humanity and to Heaven.

Lines 25–8 Ambition is my only motivation ('spur') to kill.

2 Name the deed! (in pairs)

Macbeth rarely speaks directly of killing Duncan. Instead he uses less brutal language (euphemisms): 'it', ''tis', 'assassination', 'his surcease', 'this blow', 'these cases', 'ingredience', 'the deed', 'bear the knife', 'his taking-off', 'horrid deed', 'my intent'. Read the soliloquy, saying 'killing Duncan' instead of each euphemism. Talk together about the difference the substitutions make.

---

trammel up the consequence be without consequences ('trammel' = net)

surcease death, killing

jump the life to come risk Heaven's punishment

inventor original teacher

chalice cup, goblet

faculties powers as king

cherubin angelic children

sightless couriers wind (blind or invisible runners)

no spur . . . other see page 171

Act 1 Scene 7
Macbeth's castle Near the Great Hall

Hautboys. Torches. Enter a butler and many servants with dishes and service over the stage. Then enter MACBETH

MACBETH If it were done when 'tis done, then 'twere well
It were done quickly. If th'assassination
Could trammel up the consequence and catch
With his surcease, success, that but this blow
Might be the be-all and the end-all – here,   5
But here, upon this bank and shoal of time,
We'd jump the life to come. But in these cases,
We still have judgement here that we but teach
Bloody instructions, which being taught, return
To plague th'inventor. This even-handed justice   10
Commends th'ingredience of our poisoned chalice
To our own lips. He's here in double trust:
First, as I am his kinsman and his subject,
Strong both against the deed; then, as his host,
Who should against his murderer shut the door,   15
Not bear the knife myself. Besides, this Duncan
Hath borne his faculties so meek, hath been
So clear in his great office, that his virtues
Will plead like angels, trumpet-tongued against
The deep damnation of his taking-off.   20
And pity, like a naked newborn babe
Striding the blast, or heaven's cherubin horsed
Upon the sightless couriers of the air,
Shall blow the horrid deed in every eye,
That tears shall drown the wind. I have no spur   25
To prick the sides of my intent, but only
Vaulting ambition which o'erleaps itself
And falls on th'other –

Enter LADY [MACBETH]

How now? What news?

Macbeth says he has decided not to kill Duncan. Lady Macbeth accuses him of cowardice and lack of manliness. She would kill her own child rather than break such a promise.

1 First reading (in pairs)

To gain a first impression of the power of Lady Macbeth's persuasion, take parts and speak from line 28 to the end of the scene. Make the most of Lady Macbeth's stabbing questions, taunting and contempt.

2 A wife taunts her husband (in groups of four or more)

One person reads Macbeth; all the others play Lady Macbeth. Macbeth sits or stands in the centre; the Lady Macbeths walk or stand around him. Work through lines 28–82, with each Lady Macbeth reading only up to a punctuation mark before handing on. Hurl your words at Macbeth in any manner you think appropriate.

Afterwards, discuss which sentence or phrase of Lady Macbeth's you think has the greatest effect on Macbeth in making him decide to do the murder. ('The poor cat i'th'adage' refers to a proverb about a cat who wanted a fish, but was afraid of water.)

3 Fear of being overheard (in pairs)

Both the Macbeths have left the feast they have prepared for Duncan. At any moment someone may come in and overhear their secret conversation. At what points in this scene would you advise the actors to indicate they fear being overheard? What should they do at such moments?

Not cast aside so soon   not throw away my reputation ('opinions') so quickly

so green and pale   sickly

the ornament of life   life's highest achievement (the crown)

break this enterprise   suggest killing Duncan

They have made themselves   now is the time and place to murder Duncan

fitness   timeliness

given suck   suckled a child at my breast (see page 130)

had I so sworn   if I had promised

LADY MACBETH He has almost supped. Why have you left the
            chamber?
MACBETH Hath he asked for me?
LADY MACBETH   Know you not, he has?   30
MACBETH We will proceed no further in this business.
            He hath honoured me of late, and I have bought
            Golden opinions from all sorts of people,
            Which would be worn now in their newest gloss,
            Not cast aside so soon.
LADY MACBETH   Was the hope drunk   35
            Wherein you dressed yourself? Hath it slept since?
            And wakes it now to look so green and pale
            At what it did so freely? From this time,
            Such I account thy love. Art thou afeard
            To be the same in thine own act and valour,   40
            As thou art in desire? Wouldst thou have that
            Which thou esteem'st the ornament of life,
            And live a coward in thine own esteem,
            Letting I dare not wait upon I would,
            Like the poor cat i'th'adage?
MACBETH   Prithee, peace.   45
            I dare do all that may become a man;
            Who dares do more is none.
LADY MACBETH   What beast was't then
            That made you break this enterprise to me?
            When you durst do it, then you were a man.
            And to be more than what you were, you would   50
            Be so much more the man. Nor time, nor place
            Did then adhere, and yet you would make both.
            They have made themselves and that their fitness now
            Does unmake you. I have given suck and know
            How tender 'tis to love the babe that milks me: 55
            I would, while it was smiling in my face,
            Have plucked my nipple from his boneless gums
            And dashed the brains out, had I so sworn
            As you have done to this.

Lady Macbeth will make the king's bodyguards so drunk that murdering Duncan (and blaming the bodyguards) will be easy. Macbeth applauds her. He says that they should veil their evil designs with pleasant looks.

---

1 'We fail?' (in pairs)

There are many ways of speaking these two words (incredulously, resignedly, and so on). Explore, and decide which version you prefer.

2 Evil whispers (in pairs)

Take turns to whisper Lady Macbeth's lines 59–72 to each other. The problem with whispering is that the audience cannot hear! So how, on stage, can you convey to them the sense of an evil plot being hatched?

3 Imagery

Lady Macbeth uses two metaphors familiar to Jacobean audiences:

- 'Screw your courage to the sticking-place' (line 60) suggests an archer turning the screw of his crossbow to adjust the cord to receive an arrow, or a musician tightening the strings of a violin.
- Lines 65–7 use an elaborate image from alchemy, a bogus science. Drunkenness will make the king's attendants forget their duties because noxious vapours will befuddle their reason ('memory . . . / Shall be a fume'). 'Receipt' and 'limbeck' were items of apparatus used by alchemists.

You can find more on imagery on pages 170–1.

4 'Bring forth men-children only' (in pairs)

Lady Macbeth's persuasion convinces Macbeth. He praises her bold spirit. What beliefs lie behind his lines 72–4? What do they suggest about the position of women in Scotland at the time the play is set?

---

chamberlains   attendants, bodyguards
wassail   drinking toasts ('Cheers!')
convince   overpower
drenchèd   drunken
spongy   drink-sodden

quell   slaughter, murder
mettle   spirit
receive   interpret
Each corporal agent   every part of me
mock the time   deceive the world

MACBETH   If we should fail?
LADY MACBETH   We fail?
  But screw your courage to the sticking-place,   60
  And we'll not fail. When Duncan is asleep,
  Whereto the rather shall his day's hard journey
  Soundly invite him, his two chamberlains
  Will I with wine and wassail so convince
  That memory, the warder of the brain,   65
  Shall be a fume, and the receipt of reason
  A limbeck only. When in swinish sleep
  Their drenchèd natures lies as in a death,
  What cannot you and I perform upon
  Th'unguarded Duncan? What not put upon   70
  His spongy officers, who shall bear the guilt
  Of our great quell?
MACBETH   Bring forth men-children only,
  For thy undaunted mettle should compose
  Nothing but males. Will it not be received,
  When we have marked with blood those sleepy two   75
  Of his own chamber, and used their very daggers,
  That they have done't?
LADY MACBETH   Who dares receive it other,
  As we shall make our griefs and clamour roar
  Upon his death?
MACBETH   I am settled and bend up
  Each corporal agent to this terrible feat.   80
  Away, and mock the time with fairest show,
  False face must hide what the false heart doth know.
                                                        Exeunt

Looking back at Act 1
Activities for groups or individuals

1 Contrasting scenes

Shakespeare uses the dramatic technique of juxtaposing scenes. Each scene somehow contrasts with, or comments on the preceding scene, often ironically. For example, the supernatural world of Scene 1 is followed by the military atmosphere of Scene 2. Make a list of the seven scenes of Act 1 suggesting how each dramatically contrasts with the next (for example, in terms of location, characters, action). It may help you to begin by writing a newspaper headline for each scene.

2 Appearances are deceptive

Things are not what they seem in *Macbeth*. The notion that you cannot trust outward appearances echoes through Act 1:

'Fair is foul, and foul is fair'
'nothing is but what is not'
'Look like th'innocent flower, / But be the serpent under't'
'There's no art / To find the mind's construction in the face'
'To beguile the time, look like the time'
'False face must hide what the false heart doth know'

Identify who makes each remark, and suggest why they make it. Then work out a way of presenting each line (for example, mime, tableau, drawing, paragraph of writing) to illustrate the theme of deception.

3 Witches or weird sisters?

Only once in the play does someone use the word 'witch' (see page 8). Macbeth calls them 'weird sisters'. In Anglo-Saxon mythology these were 'goddesses of destiny' who predicted the future. Find out about other supernatural beings that were believed to be dangerous or evil (for example, furies, fates, harpies, gorgons, sirens, trolls, eldritches).

4 What is 'a man'?

The idea of what it is to be 'a man' runs through the play. Make a list of eight to twelve qualities that you think 'a man' should possess. Check how many of these qualities you feel Macbeth possesses.

5 Presenting Macbeth and Lady Macbeth

There is no 'one right way' to interpret *Macbeth*. Each new production moves beyond Shakespeare's Jacobean world to express the ideas, feelings and political and social climate of its own particular time and culture:

- In 1762, David Garrick and Mrs Pritchard played in eighteenth-century costumes similar to those worn at court at the time.
- *Joe Macbeth* is set in Chicago's gangland. It follows Shakespeare's play closely, using the conventions of the gangster movie.
- *From a Jack to a King* was a 1992 rock musical adaptation of *Macbeth*.

Use the pictures below and the colour illustrations to help you write an assignment telling where you would set *Macbeth*, and how you would present Macbeth and Lady Macbeth.

Banquo tells of Duncan's gratitude for the Macbeths' hospitality. When Banquo says he has dreamt of the Witches, Macbeth replies with a lie. Banquo won't be tempted by Macbeth into betraying Duncan.

---

1 Banquo's dream

Banquo hints at the 'cursèd thoughts' that come in sleep (lines 8–9). He tells that he has dreamt of the Witches (line 20). Just what did Banquo dream? Write a story or poem entitled 'Banquo's dream'.

2 Contrast Banquo and Macbeth (in groups of three)

Shakespeare dramatises the difference between Banquo, the honourable man, and Macbeth, the deceiver. Banquo fights against evil thoughts ('Restrain in me'). He uses kind and open words in his report of Duncan. He wishes to stay free of guilt ('keep / My bosom franchised') and remain loyal ('allegiance clear') to Duncan (lines 26–9).

In sharp contrast, Macbeth speaks untruths: 'A friend'; 'Being unprepared', 'I think not of them'. He tries to tempt Banquo to his side ('cleave to my consent') in return for honour (lines 25–6).

Write advice for the actors on how to show the two men's increasingly uneasy relationship, and how to alert the audience to the contrast between them. You might find it helpful to read aloud lines 10–30, but with two people reading Macbeth (one as Macbeth, one as his evil conscience). At the end of each line Macbeth speaks, the 'evil conscience' says 'False face must hide what the false heart doth know'.

3 Fleance's point of view

Write Fleance's account of all he saw and heard in lines 1–30. What does he make of the conversation between his father and Macbeth? And what is his view of Macbeth?

---

husbandry thrift, in putting out the candles (stars)

powers angels who protect against evil

largess to your offices gifts to your servants' quarters

shut up gone to bed

Being unprepared . . . wrought the fact that Duncan's visit was unexpected meant we didn't entertain him as fully as we would have wished

Act 2 Scene 1
Macbeth's castle The courtyard

Enter BANQUO, *and* FLEANCE *with a torch-bearer before him*

BANQUO How goes the night, boy?

FLEANCE The moon is down; I have not heard the clock.

BANQUO And she goes down at twelve.

FLEANCE   I take't, 'tis later, sir.

BANQUO Hold, take my sword. – There's husbandry in heaven,

      Their candles are all out. – Take thee that too.   5

      A heavy summons lies like lead upon me,

      And yet I would not sleep; merciful powers,

      Restrain in me the cursèd thoughts that nature

      Gives way to in repose.

         Enter MACBETH, *and a Servant with a torch*

                      Give me my sword –

      Who's there?   10

MACBETH A friend.

BANQUO What, sir, not yet at rest? The king's abed.

      He hath been in unusual pleasure

      And sent forth great largess to your offices.

      This diamond he greets your wife withal,   15

         [*Gives Macbeth a diamond*]

      By the name of most kind hostess, and shut up

      In measureless content.

MACBETH   Being unprepared,

      Our will became the servant to defect,

      Which else should free have wrought.

BANQUO   All's well.

      I dreamed last night of the three weïrd sisters;   20

      To you they have showed some truth.

MACBETH   I think not of them;

      Yet when we can entreat an hour to serve,

      We would spend it in some words upon that business,

      If you would grant the time.

BANQUO   At your kind'st leisure.

MACBETH If you shall cleave to my consent, when 'tis,   25

      It shall make honour for you.

BANQUO   So I lose none

      In seeking to augment it, but still keep

      My bosom franchised and allegiance clear,

      I shall be counselled.

Alone, Macbeth hallucinates, thinking he sees a blood-stained dagger. As he moves to murder Duncan, his thoughts are filled with evil images.

1 Acting the horror (in small groups)

Macbeth's hallucination of the dagger is both a warning and an invitation. At first, his terror leads him to try to argue away the 'fatal vision', questioning the reliability of his senses. But gradually he changes his approach. Instead of resisting the horror, he intensifies it, seeing 'gouts of blood' on the dagger. He then dismisses the vision, interpreting it as created by his knowledge that he is about to murder Duncan. From line 49 he speaks what sounds like a spell or incantation, imagining a personified 'Witchcraft' at a fiendish ceremony. His comparison of himself to the rapist Tarquin adds a sinister sexual excitement to the imminent murder.

Work out your own presentation of Macbeth's soliloquy. Use some of the following points and ideas to help your thinking:

- Should a dagger actually be shown on stage (for example, as a holograph)?
- As one person reads the soliloquy a short section at a time, the others act out what Macbeth does at each moment.
- Find ways of showing Macbeth's evil imaginings in lines 49–56.
- What sound effects might you add at particular lines?
- Three people take part as the Witches and 'lead' Macbeth through the soliloquy, stage-managing affairs.

After your own presentation write a detailed account of how you would stage lines 33–64 to greatest dramatic effect.

---

sensible / To feeling able to be touched
heat-oppressèd feverish
palpable real, physical
dudgeon handle
gouts large drops

Hecate goddess of witchcraft
off'rings gifts, sacrifices
Tarquin Roman prince who raped Lucrece
prate talk
knell funeral bell

MACBETH   Good repose the while.

BANQUO Thanks, sir; the like to you.   30

> [*Exeunt*] *Banquo*[, *Fleance, and Torch-bearer*]

MACBETH [*To Servant*] Go bid thy mistress, when my drink is
    ready,
She strike upon the bell. Get thee to bed.

> *Exit* [*Servant*]

Is this a dagger which I see before me,
The handle toward my hand? Come, let me clutch thee:
I have thee not, and yet I see thee still.   35
Art thou not, fatal vision, sensible
To feeling as to sight? Or art thou but
A dagger of the mind, a false creation,
Proceeding from the heat-oppressèd brain?
I see thee yet, in form as palpable   40
As this which now I draw.
Thou marshall'st me the way that I was going,
And such an instrument I was to use.
Mine eyes are made the fools o'th'other senses,
Or else worth all the rest. I see thee still,   45
And on thy blade and dudgeon gouts of blood,
Which was not so before. There's no such thing:
It is the bloody business which informs
Thus to mine eyes. Now o'er the one half-world
Nature seems dead, and wicked dreams abuse   50
The curtained sleep. Witchcraft celebrates
Pale Hecate's off'rings, and withered murder,
Alarumed by his sentinel, the wolf,
Whose howl's his watch, thus with his stealthy pace,
With Tarquin's ravishing strides, towards his design   55
Moves like a ghost. Thou sure and firm-set earth,
Hear not my steps, which way they walk, for fear
Thy very stones prate of my whereabout,
And take the present horror from the time,
Which now suits with it. Whiles I threat, he lives;   60
Words to the heat of deeds too cold breath gives.

> *A bell rings*

I go, and it is done. The bell invites me.
Hear it not, Duncan, for it is a knell
That summons thee to heaven or to hell.   *Exit*

Lady Macbeth, exhilarated by drink, awaits Macbeth's return from Duncan's room. She has drugged Duncan's bodyguards, but fears that the murder has not been done. Macbeth returns and says he has killed the king.

1 After the murder (in pairs)

Take parts as Lady Macbeth and Macbeth. Read straight through the whole scene. (Don't pause to worry over words you are not sure of.) Then exchange roles and read through again.

a Talk together about the atmosphere of the scene and your impressions of the characters. Who is the dominant partner?

b What should be the pace of playing different sections of the scene? Write notes advising the actors where and why they might speak quickly, and where they could adopt a different style of speech.

2 Nervousness? (in pairs)

Explore different ways of staging lines 13–24 ('My husband? . . . sorry sight'). Such rapidly alternating lines are called **stichomythia**, and are usually spoken quickly on stage. Remember: it's a dark night, Macbeth has just committed a terrible killing, and the murdered king's sons are in the castle.

3 A different view of Lady Macbeth

Lady Macbeth had laid the daggers ready, but something stopped her from killing Duncan herself: 'Had he not resembled / My father as he slept, I had done't'. Choose one of the following as a title, and write a short story or poem:

- The childhood of Lady Macbeth, as told by herself
- The childhood of Lady Macbeth, as told by her father
- Lady Macbeth and the sleeping Duncan

---

quenched silenced, drugged
fatal bellman watchman who rang the bell before executions and burials
surfeited grooms drunken servants (bodyguards)

mock their charge abandon their duties
possets hot drinks
owl, crickets (both associated with death)
chamber bedroom

Act 2 Scene 2
Macbeth's castle Near Duncan's room

Enter LADY MACBETH

LADY MACBETH That which hath made them drunk, hath made
    me bold;
    What hath quenched them, hath given me fire.
                [An owl shrieks]
                                  Hark, peace!
    It was the owl that shrieked, the fatal bellman
    Which gives the stern'st good-night. He is about it.
    The doors are open, and the surfeited grooms   5
    Do mock their charge with snores. I have drugged their
      possets,
    That death and nature do contend about them,
    Whether they live, or die.

Enter MACBETH [*with two bloody daggers*]

MACBETH   Who's there? What ho?
LADY MACBETH Alack, I am afraid they have awaked,
    And 'tis not done; th'attempt and not the deed   10
    Confounds us. Hark! I laid their daggers ready,
    He could not miss 'em. Had he not resembled
    My father as he slept, I had done't. My husband?
MACBETH I have done the deed. Didst thou not hear a noise?
LADY MACBETH I heard the owl scream and the crickets cry.   15
    Did not you speak?
MACBETH When?
LADY MACBETH Now.
MACBETH As I descended?
LADY MACBETH Ay.   20
MACBETH Hark, who lies i'th'second chamber?
LADY MACBETH Donaldbain.
MACBETH This is a sorry sight.
LADY MACBETH A foolish thought, to say a sorry sight.

Macbeth is obsessed by his inability to say 'Amen', and by a voice crying that he has murdered sleep and will never sleep again. Lady Macbeth dismisses his hallucinations and orders him to return the daggers. He refuses.

1 Off stage or on stage? (in pairs)

Shakespeare chose not to show the actual killing of Duncan, perhaps to ensure that the horror of the act lies more in its moral significance than in the sight of blood. Imagine you are making a film of the play. Would you show the murder? Give reasons for your decision.

2 Conscience strikes (in pairs)

Macbeth is conscience-stricken as he struggles to say 'Amen'. His attempt to pray is thwarted. Not being able to speak the word implies that God will not bless him and he is doomed to eternal damnation. His self-condemnation continues as he thinks that he hears a voice foretelling that he will sleep no more. Many actors portray Macbeth as talking to himself, ignoring his wife. Other actors have played him feverishly telling her his story, as if she can offer help. Talk together about how you would play lines 24–46 to show how the characters relate to each other in this episode.

3 Images of sleep (in groups of four or more)

In lines 39–43 Macbeth uses vivid images to portray sleep: it 'knits up the ravelled sleeve of care', ends each day's life like death, is like a refreshing bath after heavy labour, soothes troubled minds, and is like the main course in a formal banquet. Work out a mime to show each quality. You could extend your mime by adding the results of lack of sleep promised by the First Witch in Act 1 Scene 3, lines 18–22.

---

addressed them / Again   went back
hangman's hands   blood-covered
  hands (executioners often
  disembowelled condemned men)
ravelled sleeve   frayed sleeve, or
  tangled silk

sore labour's bath   hard work's cure
Balm   healing medicine
second course   main item of a meal
unbend   relax, weaken
filthy witness   evidence (blood)
grooms   servants, bodyguards

MACBETH There's one did laugh in's sleep, and one cried,
      'Murder!',   25
    That they did wake each other; I stood, and heard them,
    But they did say their prayers and addressed them
    Again to sleep.
LADY MACBETH   There are two lodged together.
MACBETH One cried 'God bless us!' and 'Amen' the other,
    As they had seen me with these hangman's hands.   30
    List'ning their fear, I could not say 'Amen'
    When they did say 'God bless us.'
LADY MACBETH Consider it not so deeply.
MACBETH But wherefore could not I pronounce 'Amen'?
    I had most need of blessing and 'Amen'   35
    Stuck in my throat.
LADY MACBETH   These deeds must not be thought
    After these ways; so, it will make us mad.
MACBETH Methought I heard a voice cry, 'Sleep no more:
    Macbeth does murder sleep', the innocent sleep,
    Sleep that knits up the ravelled sleeve of care,   40
    The death of each day's life, sore labour's bath,
    Balm of hurt minds, great nature's second course,
    Chief nourisher in life's feast.
LADY MACBETH   What do you mean?
MACBETH Still it cried, 'Sleep no more' to all the house;
    'Glamis hath murdered sleep', and therefore Cawdor   45
    Shall sleep no more: Macbeth shall sleep no more.
LADY MACBETH Who was it, that thus cried? Why, worthy thane,
    You do unbend your noble strength to think
    So brain-sickly of things. Go get some water
    And wash this filthy witness from your hand.   50
    Why did you bring these daggers from the place?
    They must lie there. Go carry them and smear
    The sleepy grooms with blood.
MACBETH   I'll go no more.
    I am afraid to think what I have done;
    Look on't again, I dare not.

Lady Macbeth takes the daggers to smear Duncan's blood on his servants' faces. A knocking sound frightens Macbeth, but his wife tells him to pull himself together. She plans an alibi.

---

1 Wife versus husband (in pairs)

Lady Macbeth seems devoid of conscience or fear. She is concerned only to avoid blame. But as Macbeth gazes on his blood-stained hands, he is appalled to think what he has done. He feels that not all the water in the ocean can clean away Duncan's blood. Rather, his hands will make the measureless seas bloody ('multitudinous seas incarnadine').

Identify two sentences from lines 55–77 which for you express the moral difference between husband and wife in this episode.

'Give me the daggers.' How accurately do you think the expressions and postures of the Macbeths embody their feelings at this moment?

---

gild paint with blood (a pun on gild/guilt)
withal with it (blood)
Neptune god of the sea
incarnadine make blood-red

Your constancy . . . unattended you've lost your nerve
lest occasion call us in case the discovery of the murder causes us to be sent for

LADY MACBETH   Infirm of purpose!   55
    Give me the daggers. The sleeping and the dead
    Are but as pictures; 'tis the eye of childhood
    That fears a painted devil. If he do bleed,
    I'll gild the faces of the grooms withal,
    For it must seem their guilt.   *Exit*
                  Knock within
MACBETH   Whence is that knocking?   60
    How is't with me, when every noise appals me?
    What hands are here? Ha: they pluck out mine eyes.
    Will all great Neptune's ocean wash this blood
    Clean from my hand? No: this my hand will rather
    The multitudinous seas incarnadine,   65
    Making the green one red.

          Enter LADY [MACBETH]

LADY MACBETH My hands are of your colour, but I shame
    To wear a heart so white.
              Knock [within]
             I hear a knocking
    At the south entry. Retire we to our chamber;
    A little water clears us of this deed.   70
    How easy is it then! Your constancy
    Hath left you unattended.
              Knock [within]
            Hark, more knocking.
    Get on your night-gown, lest occasion call us
    And show us to be watchers. Be not lost
    So poorly in your thoughts.   75
MACBETH To know my deed, 'twere best not know my self.
              Knock [within]
    Wake Duncan with thy knocking: I would thou couldst.
                    Exeunt

Macbeth's Porter imagines himself keeper of Hell's gate. He talks about admitting to Hell a greedy farmer, a liar and a cheating tailor. He jokes with Macduff about the effects of too much drink.

1 Why include the scene? (in small groups)

Some productions cut the 'Porter scene', considering it to be irrelevant to the play. Would you present it if you were directing the play? Talk together about the case for and against including the scene. To help you, here are some of the arguments for inclusion:

Comic relief? The audience needs a space for laughter.

Time to change? The Macbeths need time to change into nightgowns.

A link with older plays? In medieval miracle plays a porter at Hell's mouth admitted sinners to the torments of Hell ('th'everlasting bonfire').

Giving a job to the comedian? Shakespeare's company, the King's Men, always included one major actor who specialised in comic parts.

Contemporary jokes? The Porter's jokes are about things that were very familiar to audiences in 1606, when the play was first performed: greedy farmers, equivocators (see page 163), cheating tailors and sexually transmitted disease ('roast your goose').

Dramatic function: echoing the play's themes? Damnation ('th'everlasting bonfire'); evil and the supernatural ('Beelzebub'); ambition (the greedy farmer); lying and deceit ('equivocator'); theft (the tailor); desire and achievement (the effects of drink).

The best test? The best way of deciding whether to include the scene is to act out lines 1–34. Try it!

2 The effects of drink (in pairs)

Invent actions ('business') that the Porter could use to accompany his list of the effects of drink (lines 23–30).

---

old   plenty of
Beelzebub   the Devil
equivocator   someone who juggles with the truth (see page 163)
French hose   baggy trousers
everlasting bonfire   eternal damnation in Hell

carousing   drinking
second cock   3 a.m.
Marry   by the Virgin Mary
mars   disables, ruins
takes him off   makes him impotent
equivocates   tricks
giving him the lie   tricking him

Act 2 Scene 3
The entrance to Macbeth's castle

Enter a PORTER. *Knocking within*

PORTER Here's a knocking indeed: if a man were porter of hell-gate, he should have old turning the key. (*Knock*) Knock, knock, knock. Who's there i'th'name of Beelzebub? Here's a farmer that hanged himself on th'expectation of plenty. Come in time – have napkins enough about you, here you'll sweat for't.   5 (*Knock*) Knock, knock. Who's there in th'other devil's name? Faith, here's an equivocator that could swear in both the scales against either scale, who committed treason enough for God's sake, yet could not equivocate to heaven. O, come in, equivocator. (*Knock*) Knock, knock, knock. Who's there? Faith,   10 here's an English tailor come hither for stealing out of a French hose. Come in, tailor, here you may roast your goose. (*Knock*) Knock, knock. Never at quiet: what are you? But this place is too cold for hell. I'll devil-porter it no further: I had thought to have let in some of all professions that go the primrose way   15 to th'everlasting bonfire. (*Knock*) Anon, anon. I pray you, remember the porter. [*Opens door*]

Enter MACDUFF *and* LENNOX

MACDUFF Was it so late, friend, ere you went to bed,
    That you do lie so late?
PORTER Faith, sir, we were carousing till the second cock, and   20 drink, sir, is a great provoker of three things.
MACDUFF What three things does drink especially provoke?
PORTER Marry, sir, nose-painting, sleep, and urine. Lechery, sir, it provokes, and unprovokes: it provokes the desire, but it takes away the performance. Therefore much drink may be said to be   25 an equivocator with lechery: it makes him, and it mars him; it sets him on, and it takes him off; it persuades him and disheartens him, makes him stand to and not stand to. In conclusion, equivocates him in a sleep, and giving him the lie, leaves him.   30

Macduff has come to meet Duncan. Macbeth shows him to Duncan's room. Lennox tells of the terrible events of the night. Horrified, Macduff returns from Duncan's room.

'Remember the porter' (Don't forget to tip me). Some actors who play the Porter ad-lib jokes about contemporary events; others exploit the sexual references to the full or tell 'knock, knock' jokes. But in nineteenth-century German productions, the Porter was a very sober figure, who sang a joyful and innocent song to welcome the sunrise. How would the Porter in your production behave?

1 A tale of horror (in small groups)

Lines 46–53 describe the terrifying night that Lennox has experienced. The earth itself seemed diseased. Nature mirrored the horror of Duncan's murder. As one person speaks Lennox's lines, the others provide appropriate sound effects.

gave thee the lie   knocked you out
requited him for his lie   paid him back for his wrestling trick
cast   throw down, or throw up (vomit)
timely   early
The labour . . . pain   the work I enjoy cures pain
limited   appointed

dire combustion   terrible fires and explosions (an echo of the Gunpowder Plot?)
obscure bird   owl (associated with death)
'Twas a rough night   (Should the audience laugh here?)

MACDUFF I believe drink gave thee the lie last night.

PORTER That it did, sir, i'the very throat on me, but I requited him for his lie, and, I think, being too strong for him, though he took up my legs sometime, yet I made a shift to cast him.

Enter MACBETH

MACDUFF Is thy master stirring? 35
    Our knocking has awaked him: here he comes.

                                           [*Exit Porter*]

LENNOX Good morrow, noble sir.

MACBETH   Good morrow, both.

MACDUFF Is the king stirring, worthy thane?

MACBETH   Not yet.

MACDUFF He did command me to call timely on him;
    I have almost slipped the hour.

MACBETH   I'll bring you to him. 40

MACDUFF I know this is a joyful trouble to you, but yet 'tis one.

MACBETH The labour we delight in physics pain. This is the door.

MACDUFF I'll make so bold to call, for 'tis my limited service.   *Exit*

LENNOX Goes the king hence today?

MACBETH He does – he did appoint so. 45

LENNOX The night has been unruly: where we lay,
    Our chimneys were blown down, and, as they say,
    Lamentings heard i'th'air, strange screams of death
    And prophesying with accents terrible
    Of dire combustion and confused events, 50
    New hatched to th'woeful time. The obscure bird
    Clamoured the livelong night. Some say, the earth
    Was feverous and did shake.

MACBETH   'Twas a rough night.

LENNOX My young remembrance cannot parallel
    A fellow to it. 55

Enter MACDUFF

MACDUFF O horror, horror, horror,
    Tongue nor heart cannot conceive, nor name thee.

MACBETH *and* LENNOX What's the matter?

Macduff, horror-struck, reveals the murder of Duncan. He tells Macbeth and Lennox to see for themselves. He shouts to awake Banquo and the king's sons. Lady Macbeth pretends concern and amazement.

---

1 'Confusion now hath made his masterpiece' (in large groups)

Macduff imagines 'Confusion' as a perverse artist who has created a 'masterpiece'. To gain a sense of the terrifying confusion that results from Duncan's murder, try this activity. You will need a large space: a hall or drama studio would be ideal, but it will work in a cleared classroom.

Everybody reads the whole page opposite, but each person begins at a different line. Start anywhere you wish in lines 59–83. As you walk around the room, greet others with a single line or sentence of the script. They will reply with a different line or sentence. Then move on to greet others. Greet as many people as you can, using a different line from the script each time.

Keep the activity going for several minutes, then meet in small groups of four or five. Read through again, taking turns to read a sentence at a time. After your activity:

a Identify as many images as you can. Suggest what each describes.

b Write notes on how to stage the lines for greatest dramatic effect.

2 'Gentle lady'?

Macduff calls Lady Macbeth 'gentle' and says the news is too cruel for a woman's hearing (lines 76–9). From your knowledge of her so far, write down six or seven adjectives to describe her that you think are more suitable than 'gentle'.

The Lord's anointed temple (Duncan)

Gorgon (from Greek mythology) Medusa, a female monstrous creature with snakes for hair; anyone who saw her was turned to stone

counterfeit imitation
The great doom's image see page 63
countenance behold, face
parley talk with
murder as it fell kill her as she heard it

MACDUFF Confusion now hath made his masterpiece:
      Most sacrilegious murder hath broke ope   60
      The Lord's anointed temple and stole thence
      The life o'th'building.
MACBETH What is't you say, the life?
LENNOX Mean you his majesty?
MACDUFF Approach the chamber and destroy your sight   65
      With a new Gorgon. Do not bid me speak:
      See and then speak yourselves.
                    Exeunt Macbeth and Lennox
                    Awake, awake!
      Ring the alarum bell! Murder and treason!
      Banquo and Donaldbain! Malcolm, awake,
      Shake off this downy sleep, death's counterfeit,   70
      And look on death itself. Up, up, and see
      The great doom's image. Malcolm, Banquo,
      As from your graves rise up and walk like sprites
      To countenance this horror.

        Bell rings. Enter LADY [MACBETH]

LADY MACBETH   What's the business
      That such a hideous trumpet calls to parley   75
      The sleepers of the house? Speak, speak.
MACDUFF   O gentle lady,
      'Tis not for you to hear what I can speak.
      The repetition in a woman's ear
      Would murder as it fell. –

        Enter BANQUO

                O Banquo, Banquo,
      Our royal master's murdered.
LADY MACBETH   Woe, alas.   80
      What, in our house?
BANQUO   Too cruel, anywhere.
      Dear Duff, I prithee contradict thyself
      And say it is not so.

Macbeth says that Duncan's death empties the world of meaning. Duncan's sons are told the news of their father's murder. Macbeth defends his killing of the bodyguards. Lady Macbeth faints and is carried out.

1 Does he sound sincere? (in pairs)

Macbeth's two longer speeches opposite show how he uses elaborate imagery to try to persuade others and conceal the truth.

In lines 84–9 Macbeth says that Duncan's death makes trivial ('toys') everything worthwhile in life ('renown and grace'). Duncan was 'The wine of life' and everyone else in the world is far inferior ('the mere lees') – but it was Macbeth himself who killed Duncan.

In lines 101–11 Macbeth defends his killing of Duncan's attendants. He uses language rich in evocative imagery ('silver', 'golden', 'trade', 'Unmannerly breeched') – but he knows that what he says is false.

Read both speeches to each other several times. Talk together about whether Macbeth sounds sincere or insincere. Look ahead to lines 129–30 to discover if your view matches Malcolm's.

2 'O, by whom?' (in groups of eight)

Who has done the murder? Only two people on stage know the truth. Take parts and prepare a tableau of line 93 to show just how everyone looks at the moment when Malcolm asks his question. Who is suspicious of whom? Who looks at whom, and who avoids eye-contact? Compare the tableaux of each group, identifying who's who and their suspicions.

3 Does she really faint? (in groups of four)

Is Lady Macbeth's swoon genuine or not? Two people argue that it's real; two argue that it's faked.

---

mortality human destiny or life
drawn finished, empty
lees dregs (as in a wine glass)
vault world (with a pun on wine vault?)
temp'rate even-tempered

Th'expedition the haste
the pauser, reason delaying thought
Unmannerly breeched rudely covered
gore blood

Enter MACBETH *and* LENNOX

MACBETH Had I but died an hour before this chance,
I had lived a blessèd time, for from this instant,   85
There's nothing serious in mortality.
All is but toys; renown and grace is dead,
The wine of life is drawn, and the mere lees
Is left this vault to brag of.

Enter MALCOLM *and* DONALDBAIN

DONALDBAIN What is amiss?
MACBETH   You are, and do not know't.   90
The spring, the head, the fountain of your blood
Is stopped, the very source of it is stopped.
MACDUFF Your royal father's murdered.
MALCOLM   O, by whom?
LENNOX Those of his chamber, as it seemed, had done't.
Their hands and faces were all badged with blood,   95
So were their daggers which, unwiped, we found
Upon their pillows. They stared and were distracted;
No man's life was to be trusted with them.
MACBETH O, yet I do repent me of my fury
That I did kill them.
MACDUFF   Wherefore did you so?   100
MACBETH Who can be wise, amazed, temp'rate, and furious,
Loyal and neutral, in a moment? No man.
Th'expedition of my violent love
Outran the pauser, reason. Here lay Duncan,
His silver skin laced with his golden blood   105
And his gashed stabs looked like a breach in nature,
For ruin's wasteful entrance. There the murderers,
Steeped in the colours of their trade; their daggers
Unmannerly breeched with gore. Who could refrain,
That had a heart to love and in that heart   110
Courage to make's love known?
LADY MACBETH   Help me hence, ho.
MACDUFF Look to the lady.

[*Exit Lady Macbeth, helped*]

Donaldbain and Malcolm fear for their future. Banquo and the others swear to investigate the murder. Duncan's sons, suspecting danger, resolve to flee: Malcolm to England, Donaldbain to Ireland.

---

1 Banquo and Macbeth: another contrast

What do the declarations of Banquo ('In the great hand of God I stand', line 123) and Macbeth ('put on manly readiness', line 126) suggest to you about the differences in their characters?

2 'There's daggers in men's smiles' (in small groups)

Yet again the theme of deceptive appearance is heard. Present line 133 in the most imaginative way you can. Find two other lines opposite which express the same idea and remind yourself of other lines earlier in the play which also do so (see page 36).

3 But are they sensible? (in pairs)

Malcolm and Donaldbain don't wish to join with ('consort') the other thanes. They fear that their kinsmen are likely to murder them: 'the nea'er . . . bloody' (lines 133–4). Stealing away in these circumstances is legitimate 'theft': 'There's warrant . . . left' (lines 138–9). But do you think they take the most sensible decision? Compile as many reasons as you can for and against their decision to flee.

4 Investigating the murder (in groups of five)

Banquo proposes a meeting to investigate the murder. Everyone is under suspicion. The meeting is not shown on stage. Carry out your own enquiry by taking parts as Macbeth, Lady Macbeth, Banquo, Macduff and the Porter (Malcolm and Donaldbain have already fled). One by one, each character is questioned by everyone else about their actions, their knowledge and their suspicions.

---

auger hole tiny hole
tears grief
brewed matured into what to do
upon the foot of motion ready to express
naked frailties unclothed bodies (or weak feelings)

scruples doubts
undivulged pretence hidden purposes
an office a duty
shaft arrow
lighted hit its target
shift away leave instantly

MALCOLM [*To Donaldbain*] Why do we hold our tongues, that
      most may claim
    This argument for ours?
DONALDBAIN [*To Malcolm*]   What should be spoken here,
    Where our fate hid in an auger hole may rush   115
    And seize us? Let's away. Our tears are not yet brewed.
MALCOLM [*To Donaldbain*] Nor our strong sorrow upon the foot
      of motion.
BANQUO Look to the lady,
    And when we have our naked frailties hid
    That suffer in exposure, let us meet   120
    And question this most bloody piece of work
    To know it further. Fears and scruples shake us:
    In the great hand of God I stand and thence
    Against the undivulged pretence I fight
    Of treasonous malice.
MACDUFF   And so do I.
ALL   So all.   125
MACBETH Let's briefly put on manly readiness
    And meet i'th'hall together.
ALL   Well contented.
      Exeunt [all but Malcolm and Donaldbain]
MALCOLM What will you do? Let's not consort with them.
    To show an unfelt sorrow is an office
    Which the false man does easy. I'll to England.   130
DONALDBAIN To Ireland, I. Our separated fortune
    Shall keep us both the safer. Where we are,
    There's daggers in men's smiles; the nea'er in blood,
    The nearer bloody.
MALCOLM   This murderous shaft that's shot
    Hath not yet lighted, and our safest way   135
    Is to avoid the aim. Therefore to horse,
    And let us not be dainty of leave-taking,
    But shift away. There's warrant in that theft
    Which steals itself when there's no mercy left.
      Exeunt

Ross and an Old Man talk about the darkness and unnaturalness of events that mirror Duncan's murder. The sun is obscured, owls kill falcons, and Duncan's horses eat each other. Macduff arrives.

1 Unnatural acts (in pairs)

Darkness in daytime, owls killing falcons, horses eating each other: these strange and terrible disruptions in nature mirror the chaos of the social world – Macbeth's murder of Duncan. Improvise further conversation between Ross and the Old Man in which they describe other bizarre events that reflect the consequences of the murder.

2 Who is the Old Man?

This is the Old Man's only appearance in the play. His dramatic function is rather like the chorus in a Greek tragedy. There, the chorus comments on the action, shows its universality (how the action is reflected in nature and society), and represents the point of view of the ordinary people.

First, decide whether the Old Man fulfils those three functions as a kind of chorus. Then consider him as a character who has grown old under the rule of the feuding war-lords of Scotland. Write his autobiography, remembering he has seen 'Hours dreadful and things strange' (line 3).

3 Ross: can you believe him? (in pairs)

Ross is a thane, a high-ranking nobleman. Did he really see Duncan's horses eating each other? Suggest one or two possible reasons why he claims to have seen such an improbable sight. (In Roman Polanski's film, Ross was played as a devious character.)

Threescore and ten   seventy years
Hath trifled former knowings   has
  made past events seem trivial
heavens/act/stage   (theatrical
  metaphors)

travelling lamp   sun
the day's shame   Duncan's murder
entomb   bury
minions   favourites, the best
Contending   rebelling

Act 2 Scene 4
Outside Macbeth's castle

Enter ROSS, *with an* OLD MAN

OLD MAN Threescore and ten I can remember well;
   Within the volume of which time, I have seen
   Hours dreadful and things strange, but this sore night
   Hath trifled former knowings.
ROSS   Ha, good father,
   Thou seest the heavens, as troubled with man's act,   5
   Threatens his bloody stage. By th'clock 'tis day
   And yet dark night strangles the travelling lamp.
   Is't night's predominance, or the day's shame,
   That darkness does the face of earth entomb
   When living light should kiss it?
OLD MAN   'Tis unnatural,   10
   Even like the deed that's done. On Tuesday last,
   A falcon tow'ring in her pride of place
   Was by a mousing owl hawked at and killed.
ROSS And Duncan's horses, a thing most strange and certain,
   Beauteous and swift, the minions of their race,   15
   Turned wild in nature, broke their stalls, flung out,
   Contending 'gainst obedience as they would
   Make war with mankind.
OLD MAN   'Tis said, they eat each other.
ROSS They did so, to th'amazement of mine eyes
   That looked upon't.

Enter MACDUFF

      Here comes the good Macduff.   20
  How goes the world, sir, now?
MACDUFF   Why, see you not?

Macduff tells that Duncan's sons bribed the killers and have now fled. Macbeth has been elected king, and has gone to Scone to be crowned. Macduff will not attend the ceremony. The Old Man blesses peacemakers.

---

1 Macbeth's Scotland

a Make your own map of Scotland and design pictures or emblems to illustrate the various locations.

b Find out all you can about Scone and Iona (Colmkill). In addition to the historical facts you discover, include in your report a section on the symbolic significance of these two places in the play.

'Where the place?' The map shows the locations of the play. It also shows the rough locations of the territories of the thanes.

---

suborned bribed (to murder Duncan)
Thriftless greedy
ravin up devour
named elected king by the thanes (see page 62)

Scone a palace near Perth, where Kings of Scotland were crowned
Colmkill Iona, the traditional burial place of Kings of Scotland
Fife Macduff's territory
benison blessing

ROSS Is't known who did this more than bloody deed?

MACDUFF Those that Macbeth hath slain.

ROSS   Alas the day,
        What good could they pretend?

MACDUFF   They were suborned.
        Malcolm and Donaldbain, the king's two sons,   25
        Are stol'n away and fled, which puts upon them
        Suspicion of the deed.

ROSS   'Gainst nature still.
        Thriftless ambition that will ravin up
        Thine own life's means. Then 'tis most like
        The sovereignty will fall upon Macbeth.   30

MACDUFF He is already named and gone to Scone
        To be invested.

ROSS Where is Duncan's body?

MACDUFF   Carried to Colmkill,
        The sacred storehouse of his predecessors
        And guardian of their bones.

ROSS   Will you to Scone?   35

MACDUFF No, cousin, I'll to Fife.

ROSS   Well, I will thither.

MACDUFF Well may you see things well done there. Adieu,
        Lest our old robes sit easier than our new.

ROSS Farewell, father.

OLD MAN God's benison go with you, and with those   40
        That would make good of bad, and friends of foes.

                                                        Exeunt

Looking back at Act 2
Activities for groups and individuals

---

1 Imagery of violence

Much of the imagery in Act 2 is of violence, horror, and disruption in nature. Identify one such image that you think is especially powerful from each of the four scenes. Write a brief account of the effect of each image: what atmosphere it creates or what it reveals about a character.

2 A servant's tale

Imagine that you are one of Macbeth's servants at Inverness. You have watched Macbeth's behaviour since he returned from the wars, and overheard snatches of what he and Lady Macbeth said. Write a letter home to tell what you know.

3 The election of Macbeth as king

In the eleventh century, Kings of Scotland were elected by their fellow thanes. The title did not automatically descend from father to son. As the family tree below shows, Macbeth had a strong claim to be king, both in his own right and through his wife (granddaughter of a former high king). What happened at the meeting (not shown by Shakespeare) when Macbeth was 'named' as king? Were there

Reigns of High Kings of Scotland

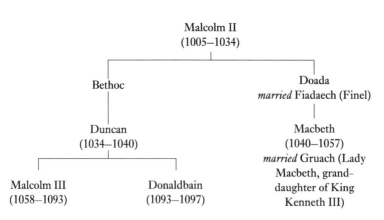

arguments over his right to succeed? Did anyone speak up for the claims of Malcolm or Donaldbain? Improvise the meeting of the Scottish thanes that resulted in the election of Macbeth.

4 Shakespeare's memory?

When Macduff shouts 'Up, up, and see / The great doom's image' (Scene 3, lines 71–2), is Shakespeare recalling his schooldays? The vision of the Day of Judgement is painted on the wall of the Guild Chapel in Stratford-upon-Avon, next door to Shakespeare's school. As a schoolboy he must have seen the painting often. Similar wall-paintings (called dooms) were in many churches. They showed all the dead rising from their graves on the Last Day to be judged and sent to either Heaven or Hell. If you go to Stratford-upon-Avon, go into the Guild Chapel and look at the doom with lines 71–4 in your mind.

Banquo fears that Macbeth has become king by evil means, but he takes heart from the Witches' predictions for his own descendants. Macbeth requests Banquo to attend tonight's banquet.

'Thou hast it now, King, Cawdor, Glamis, all.' Macbeth now wears the crown of Scotland, but what does his face reveal of his 'mind's construction'?

---

stand in thy posterity remain in your family
verities truths
made good proved

oracles prophets
Sennet trumpet call (of seven notes)
all thing unbecoming totally inappropriate

Act 3 Scene 1
The royal palace at Forres

Enter BANQUO *dressed for riding*

BANQUO Thou hast it now, King, Cawdor, Glamis, all,
As the weïrd women promised, and I fear
Thou played'st most foully for't; yet it was said
It should not stand in thy posterity,
But that myself should be the root and father   5
Of many kings. If there come truth from them –
As upon thee, Macbeth, their speeches shine –
Why by the verities on thee made good,
May they not be my oracles as well
And set me up in hope? But hush, no more.   10

Sennet sounded. Enter MACBETH *as King,* LADY [MACBETH *as
Queen*], LENNOX, ROSS, *Lords, and Attendants*

MACBETH Here's our chief guest.
LADY MACBETH   If he had been forgotten,
It had been as a gap in our great feast
And all thing unbecoming.
MACBETH Tonight we hold a solemn supper, sir,
And I'll request your presence.
BANQUO   Let your highness   15
Command upon me, to the which my duties
Are with a most indissoluble tie
Forever knit.

Macbeth claims that Duncan's sons are spreading malicious rumours. He checks that Fleance will ride this afternoon with Banquo, then dismisses the court. A servant confirms two men (the Murderers) are waiting.

1 Macbeth hides his evil intentions (in pairs)

Macbeth flatters Banquo as a valued adviser. He questions Banquo closely about his intention to ride this afternoon. But Macbeth has evil intentions for his friend, hidden behind his apparently well-meaning words. For example, Macbeth's order 'Fail not our feast' is deeply ironic, because Macbeth intends that Banquo will never arrive, having been murdered at Macbeth's command.

One person reads slowly all Macbeth's words in lines 11–41. The other says 'false face' every time he says something insincere – and adds what is really on Macbeth's mind!

2 'Strange invention' (in pairs)

What was the 'strange invention' (terrible lies) that Macbeth says Duncan's sons are spreading? Such claims could have been spread by handbills or posters. Step into role as Malcolm and Donaldbain and write the text for a handbill, putting your side of the story.

3 Why is Lady Macbeth dismissed?

In many productions, Lady Macbeth approaches Macbeth at line 45, obviously wanting to talk, but is shocked to be dismissed with 'While then, God be with you.'

Why does Macbeth send his wife away with the rest of the court? Is the evil they have committed beginning to drive them apart? Imagine you are Lady Macbeth. Write a diary entry that reports your feelings and thoughts about why you were sent away.

---

still always
grave and prosperous wise and helpful
Go not my horse the better If my horse isn't speedy
parricide father's murder

strange invention terrible lies, rumours
Craving us jointly requiring the attention of both of us
Hie you hurry
without outside

MACBETH Ride you this afternoon?

BANQUO Ay, my good lord.   20

MACBETH We should have else desired your good advice
       Which still hath been both grave and prosperous
       In this day's council: but we'll take tomorrow.
       Is't far you ride?

BANQUO As far, my lord, as will fill up the time   25
       'Twixt this and supper. Go not my horse the better,
       I must become a borrower of the night
       For a dark hour, or twain.

MACBETH Fail not our feast.

BANQUO My lord, I will not.   30

MACBETH We hear our bloody cousins are bestowed
       In England and in Ireland, not confessing
       Their cruel parricide, filling their hearers
       With strange invention. But of that tomorrow,
       When therewithal we shall have cause of state   35
       Craving us jointly. Hie you to horse; adieu,
       Till you return at night. Goes Fleance with you?

BANQUO Ay, my good lord; our time does call upon's.

MACBETH I wish your horses swift and sure of foot,
       And so I do commend you to their backs.   40
       Farewell.

                                  Exit Banquo

       Let every man be master of his time
       Till seven at night; to make society
       The sweeter welcome, we will keep ourself
       Till supper-time alone. While then, God be with you.   45

              Exeunt [all but Macbeth and a Servant]

       Sirrah, a word with you: attend those men
       Our pleasure?

SERVANT They are, my lord, without the palace gate.

Macbeth broods on his fears that Banquo's descendants will become kings. The two Murderers enter, and Macbeth reminds them of an earlier conversation when he told them that Banquo is their enemy.

1 Thoughts of Banquo (in pairs)

As he waits for the Murderers, Macbeth reveals how much he fears Banquo. His dispirited soliloquy begins with the thought that it is nothing to be king ('thus') unless he is safely king. He acknowledges Banquo's integrity, but feels that Banquo is like a thorn in his flesh (just as, in Ancient Rome, Mark Antony was said to be in fear of Octavius Caesar). Macbeth finds his own achievement is 'fruitless' and 'barren'. He has damaged his soul ('mine eternal jewel') simply to make Banquo's descendants kings. He decides to challenge the Witches' prophecies and to take action against the man he now hates.

To experience how much Macbeth now detests Banquo, try this: one person reads the soliloquy, the other echoes any word referring to Banquo (his name, 'he', 'his', 'him') in an angry voice and any word referring to Macbeth ('I', 'my', 'me') in a complaining voice.

2 Yesterday: 'Our last conference' (in groups of three)

Macbeth has had an earlier meeting with the Murderers. He told them ('passed in probation with you') that Banquo has deceived them ('borne in hand'), and it was all Banquo's doing that they were so poor and out of luck ('held you so under fortune'). Improvise that earlier conversation as Macbeth lays all the blame on Banquo. Take lines 77–83 and 85–9 as your starting point.

---

thus king
dauntless fearless
genius guardian angel
chid chided, challenged
gripe grasp
with an unlineal hand by someone
 not of my family
issue descendants

filed defiled
rancours bitterness, poison
eternal jewel immortal soul
seeds descendants
list jousting tournament, battlefield
utterance death
crossed double-crossed

MACBETH Bring them before us.

Exit Servant

       To be thus is nothing,
But to be safely thus. Our fears in Banquo   50
Stick deep, and in his royalty of nature
Reigns that which would be feared. 'Tis much he dares,
And to that dauntless temper of his mind,
He hath a wisdom that doth guide his valour
To act in safety. There is none but he,   55
Whose being I do fear; and under him
My genius is rebuked, as it is said
Mark Antony's was by Caesar. He chid the sisters
When first they put the name of king upon me
And bade them speak to him. Then prophet-like, 60
They hailed him father to a line of kings.
Upon my head they placed a fruitless crown
And put a barren sceptre in my gripe,
Thence to be wrenched with an unlineal hand,
No son of mine succeeding. If't be so,   65
For Banquo's issue have I filed my mind;
For them, the gracious Duncan have I murdered,
Put rancours in the vessel of my peace
Only for them, and mine eternal jewel
Given to the common enemy of man,   70
To make them kings, the seeds of Banquo kings.
Rather than so, come Fate into the list,
And champion me to th'utterance. Who's there?

   Enter Servant and two MURDERERS

[*To Servant*] Now go to the door and stay there till we call.

Exit Servant

Was it not yesterday we spoke together?   75
MURDERERS It was, so please your highness.
MACBETH Well then, now have you considered of my speeches?
  Know, that it was he in the times past which held you so under
  fortune, which you thought had been our innocent self. This I
  made good to you in our last conference; passed in probation 80
  with you how you were borne in hand, how crossed; the instruments, who wrought with them, and all things else that might to
  half a soul and to a notion crazed say, 'Thus did Banquo.'

Macbeth taunts the Murderers, urging them to show they are men, not dogs. If they can prove their manhood, he will help them to kill Banquo. The Murderers claim that they are so desperate they'll do anything.

1 Men and dogs (in pairs)

Just as Lady Macbeth had questioned Macbeth's manhood, he now similarly needles the Murderers. Are they just 'men', or do they have particular qualities that mark them out as really worthy? He gives a random list of dogs ('shoughs' and 'water-rugs' are long-haired dogs; 'demi-wolves' are a cross between dogs and wolves). Macbeth then lists the dogs' more important qualities ('slow', 'subtle', and so on) by which their worth is judged, and says that men can similarly be ranked by their qualities.

Try reading lines 91–100 as one long sneer; then explore other ways of speaking them.

2 What's made them so bitter? (in groups of three)

Life has embittered the two Murderers (lines 107–13). One doesn't care what he does to spite the world; the other will do anything, even if it results in his death. What is it about the Scotland of the time that has made them like this? One person interviews the two Murderers. Afterwards, write up their life stories.

3 Staging the meeting

A king is meeting two very low-status subjects. He wants them to perform a murder for him. Write notes on how you would stage the episode. Is Macbeth seated, or does he walk around the two men? Do the two men stand close together for reassurance, or . . . ? Identify movement, expressions and gestures throughout the encounter.

---

so gospelled   such believers in the Christian doctrine of forgiving your enemies
the catalogue   the list
clept   called
valued file   a list arranged by valued qualities

Particular addition   distinctive qualities
bill   list, label
station in the file   place in the list of valued people (or soldiers)
put that . . . bosoms   reveal a plan to you

FIRST MURDERER You made it known to us.

MACBETH I did so, and went further, which is now our point of 85
second meeting. Do you find your patience so predominant in
your nature, that you can let this go? Are you so gospelled, to
pray for this good man and for his issue, whose heavy hand
hath bowed you to the grave and beggared yours forever?

FIRST MURDERER We are men, my liege. 90

MACBETH Ay, in the catalogue ye go for men,
As hounds, and greyhounds, mongrels, spaniels, curs,
Shoughs, water-rugs, and demi-wolves are clept
All by the name of dogs. The valued file
Distinguishes the swift, the slow, the subtle, 95
The housekeeper, the hunter, every one
According to the gift which bounteous nature
Hath in him closed, whereby he does receive
Particular addition from the bill
That writes them all alike. And so of men. 100
Now, if you have a station in the file
Not i'th'worst rank of manhood, say't,
And I will put that business in your bosoms,
Whose execution takes your enemy off,
Grapples you to the heart and love of us 105
Who wear our health but sickly in his life,
Which in his death were perfect.

SECOND MURDERER   I am one, my liege,
Whom the vile blows and buffets of the world
Hath so incensed that I am reckless what I do
To spite the world.

FIRST MURDERER   And I another, 110
So weary with disasters, tugged with fortune,
That I would set my life on any chance
To mend it or be rid on't.

MACBETH   Both of you know
Banquo was your enemy.

MURDERERS   True, my lord.

Macbeth says that Banquo is his enemy, but he cannot kill him openly. He will arrange a time and place for the Murderers to assassinate Banquo and Fleance so that no suspicion falls upon himself.

---

1 An invitation to murder (in pairs)

Why doesn't Macbeth simply order the Murderers to do the killing? He is the king and has great power. Instead, he talks with them at some length, and gives several of his reasons. Why?

First, try out several ways of speaking Macbeth's lines opposite (for example, friendly, threateningly, confidentially, anxiously). Then write a few reasons why you think Shakespeare presents the scene in this way, rather than have Macbeth simply issue a command.

2 An interruption (in pairs)

Macbeth cuts off the First Murderer at line 127. How should he speak 'Your spirits shine through you', and what does it suggest about his opinion of the two men?

3 Killing the killers (in pairs)

Compare the two final lines (140–1) with Macbeth's last two lines before he murdered Duncan (Act 2 Scene 1, lines 63–4). Imagine that he intends to kill the two Murderers after they have murdered Banquo. Write two lines in the same style of these two couplets in which Macbeth reveals his intention to kill the killers.

4 Macbeth's morality

Like all tyrants, Macbeth hires thugs and villains to do his dirty work for him. Write a paragraph saying how you think Macbeth's moral condition seems to have changed from earlier scenes.

---

distance   enmity, quarrel (distance between swordsmen)
near'st of life   very existence
bid my will avouch it   justify it by my desires
the common eye   public view
perfect spy o'th'time   exact information

something from   away from
clearness   freedom from suspicion
rubs   roughnesses
botches   bungling
absence   death, murder
material   important
anon   immediately

MACBETH So is he mine, and in such bloody distance   115
        That every minute of his being thrusts
        Against my near'st of life; and though I could
        With barefaced power sweep him from my sight
        And bid my will avouch it, yet I must not,
        For certain friends that are both his and mine,   120
        Whose loves I may not drop, but wail his fall
        Who I myself struck down. And thence it is
        That I to your assistance do make love,
        Masking the business from the common eye
        For sundry weighty reasons.
SECOND MURDERER   We shall, my lord,   125
        Perform what you command us.
FIRST MURDERER   Though our lives –
MACBETH Your spirits shine through you. Within this hour at
          most,
        I will advise you where to plant yourselves,
        Acquaint you with the perfect spy o'th'time,
        The moment on't, for't must be done tonight,   130
        And something from the palace: always thought,
        That I require a clearness. And with him,
        To leave no rubs nor botches in the work,
        Fleance, his son that keeps him company,
        Whose absence is no less material to me   135
        Than is his father's, must embrace the fate
        Of that dark hour. Resolve yourselves apart,
        I'll come to you anon.
MURDERERS   We are resolved, my lord.
MACBETH I'll call upon you straight; abide within.
                    [*Exeunt Murderers*]
        It is concluded. Banquo, thy soul's flight,   140
        If it find heaven, must find it out tonight.   *Exit*

Lady Macbeth is troubled. She advises Macbeth not to brood on what's done, but he is still racked by fears and insecurity. He even envies the peace of death that Duncan enjoys.

---

1 Apocalypse now: what dreams? (in pairs)

Lady Macbeth seems weary and isolated. Becoming queen has brought only loss of contentment. She thinks her husband is even more emotionally troubled, full of 'sorriest fancies'. In his speech to her, he uses an apocalyptic image that visualises the universe shattering, and Heaven and Earth in anguish: 'let the frame of things disjoint, both the worlds suffer', and tells of the terrible dreams that torment him every night. What were those dreams? Improvise Macbeth on the psychoanalyst's couch, telling of his dreams.

2 'What's done, is done' (in small groups)

Take no notice of things in the past – they can't be changed or cured – advises Lady Macbeth. Do you think Macbeth can accept that advice? Can he simply disregard or forget the past? Talk together about whether you agree with what Lady Macbeth says in lines 11–12. You could use examples from your own experience to support your view.

3 The language of unease (in pairs)

Shakespeare uses the technique of antithesis (the opposition of words or phrases against each other in balanced contrast) to express Lady Macbeth's uneasy feelings and Macbeth's troubled conscience. Antithesis often creates a seesaw rhythm, as in 'Nought's had, all's spent', 'our desire . . . without content'. Explore lines 4–26 to find as many of these 'oppositions' as you can. Make a list of them and talk together about how they express the Macbeths' mental state. (You will find more on antithesis on pages 171–2.)

Nought's had, all's spent
nothing's gained, everything's lost
sorriest fancies miserable
imaginings
close, and be herself join together
again

poor malice weak deeds (to gain the crown)
let the frame of things disjoint
let the universe shatter
Malice domestic civil war
foreign levy foreign armies

Act 3 Scene 2
A room in Macbeth's palace

Enter LADY MACBETH, *and a* SERVANT

LADY MACBETH Is Banquo gone from court?

SERVANT Ay, madam, but returns again tonight.

LADY MACBETH Say to the king, I would attend his leisure
For a few words.

SERVANT   Madam, I will.   *Exit*

LADY MACBETH   Nought's had, all's spent
Where our desire is got without content.   5
'Tis safer to be that which we destroy
Than by destruction dwell in doubtful joy.

Enter MACBETH

How now, my lord, why do you keep alone,
Of sorriest fancies your companions making,
Using those thoughts which should indeed have died   10
With them they think on? Things without all remedy
Should be without regard; what's done, is done.

MACBETH We have scorched the snake, not killed it;
She'll close, and be herself, whilst our poor malice
Remains in danger of her former tooth.   15
But let the frame of things disjoint, both the worlds suffer,
Ere we will eat our meal in fear, and sleep
In the affliction of these terrible dreams
That shake us nightly. Better be with the dead
Whom we, to gain our peace, have sent to peace,   20
Than on the torture of the mind to lie
In restless ecstasy. Duncan is in his grave.
After life's fitful fever, he sleeps well;
Treason has done his worst; nor steel nor poison,
Malice domestic, foreign levy, nothing   25
Can touch him further.

Macbeth tells his wife to pay special regard to Banquo at the banquet. He speaks contemptuously of having to flatter deceitfully. He hints darkly that terrible deeds will be performed that night.

---

1 Echoes of evil (in pairs)

Macbeth's lines 40–53 ('ere . . . rouse') use terrifyingly intense images. They echo his 'dagger' soliloquy and Lady Macbeth's invocation to evil in Act 1 Scene 5, lines 38–52. He sounds like a witch performing a horrible ritual. Take turns to speak the lines to create a chillingly dramatic atmosphere.

'O, full of scorpions is my mind, dear wife!' Pick out other lines from this scene that could make a suitable caption for the picture.

Sleek   smooth
present him eminence   praise and honour him
unsafe the while   it's still a dangerous time for us
lave   wash
vizards   masks

Nature's copy's not eterne   life doesn't last for ever
Hecate   goddess of witchcraft
shard-born   flying (shard = wing covers)
seeling   blinding (hawks' eyes were 'seeled' by sewing them up)

LADY MACBETH Come on. Gentle my lord,
   Sleek o'er your rugged looks, be bright and jovial
   Among your guests tonight.
MACBETH   So shall I, love,
   And so I pray be you. Let your remembrance   30
   Apply to Banquo, present him eminence
   Both with eye and tongue; unsafe the while, that we
   Must lave our honours in these flattering streams
   And make our faces vizards to our hearts,
   Disguising what they are.
LADY MACBETH   You must leave this.   35
MACBETH O, full of scorpions is my mind, dear wife!
   Thou know'st that Banquo and his Fleance lives.
LADY MACBETH But in them Nature's copy's not eterne.
MACBETH There's comfort yet, they are assailable;
   Then be thou jocund: ere the bat hath flown   40
   His cloistered flight, ere to black Hecate's summons
   The shard-born beetle with his drowsy hums
   Hath rung night's yawning peal, there shall be done
   A deed of dreadful note.
LADY MACBETH   What's to be done?
MACBETH Be innocent of the knowledge, dearest chuck,   45
   Till thou applaud the deed. Come, seeling night,
   Scarf up the tender eye of pitiful day
   And with thy bloody and invisible hand
   Cancel and tear to pieces that great bond
   Which keeps me pale. Light thickens,   50
   And the crow makes wing to th'rooky wood;
   Good things of day begin to droop and drowse,
   Whiles night's black agents to their preys do rouse.
   Thou marvell'st at my words, but hold thee still;
   Things bad begun, make strong themselves by ill.   55
   So prithee, go with me.
                Exeunt

A third Murderer has joined the other two to await their victims. They kill Banquo, but Fleance escapes.

---

1 Act out the scene! (in groups of five)

This very short scene is full of action. It takes place in darkness, but the audience must be able to see exactly what happens. Take parts and act out the scene. A hint: slow motion rehearsals of the attack are helpful, both for working out the movements and for safety reasons.

2 Why a Third Murderer? (in pairs)

Why has Macbeth sent along another Murderer? Talk together about possible reasons. In some productions he is Macbeth himself, in disguise (but that is unlikely because of Macbeth's behaviour in the next scene).

3 Write a dying speech for Banquo (in pairs)

In many of his earlier plays, Shakespeare gave long emotional speeches to dying men. But in *Macbeth* he doesn't do that. Talk together about possible reasons why Shakespeare did not write dying speeches for Duncan and Banquo (and Macbeth himself).

Invent a dying speech for Banquo. Write it in Shakespearian-style verse if you can. Think of all the things Banquo might have said if he'd been given time.

4 A poetic murderer?

Some people have found it curious that the First Murderer speaks lines 5–7 ('The west . . . inn'). They feel that such 'poetic' language is inappropriate in the mouth of a common murderer. Why do you think Shakespeare gives him this language style here?

---

offices   duties
To the direction just   precisely
spurs the lated   gallops the late
The subject of our watch   the person we are waiting for

within the note of expectation   on the list of expected guests
go about   turn back
best half of our affair   half our reward (or half our task)

Act 3 Scene 3
A lonely place near Forres

Enter three MURDERERS

FIRST MURDERER But who did bid thee join with us?

THIRD MURDERER   Macbeth.

SECOND MURDERER He needs not our mistrust, since he delivers
   Our offices and what we have to do
   To the direction just.

FIRST MURDERER [*To Third Murderer*] Then stand with us.
   The west yet glimmers with some streaks of day;   5
   Now spurs the lated traveller apace
   To gain the timely inn, and near approaches
   The subject of our watch.

THIRD MURDERER   Hark, I hear horses.

BANQUO (*Within*) Give us a light there, ho!

SECOND MURDERER   Then 'tis he; the rest
   That are within the note of expectation   10
   Already are i'th'court.

FIRST MURDERER   His horses go about.

THIRD MURDERER Almost a mile; but he does usually,
   So all men do, from hence to th'palace gate
   Make it their walk.

Enter BANQUO *and* FLEANCE, *with a torch*

SECOND MURDERER A light, a light!   15

THIRD MURDERER 'Tis he.

FIRST MURDERER Stand to't.

BANQUO It will be rain tonight.

FIRST MURDERER   Let it come down.
  [*The Murderers attack. First Murderer strikes out the light*]

BANQUO O, treachery!
   Fly, good Fleance, fly, fly, fly!   20
   Thou mayst revenge – O slave! [*Dies. Fleance escapes*]

THIRD MURDERER Who did strike out the light?

FIRST MURDERER   Was't not the way?

THIRD MURDERER There's but one down; the son is fled.

SECOND MURDERER We have lost best half of our affair.

FIRST MURDERER Well, let's away, and say how much is done.   25
      Exeunt[, *with Banquo's body*]

Macbeth welcomes his guests to the banquet and mixes with them. The First Murderer reports Banquo's death. The news of Fleance's escape disturbs Macbeth and renews his fears.

---

1 'Play the humble host'

Scene 4 dramatises a feast. In warrior Scotland such a banquet expressed harmony between a king and his subjects. But Macbeth has violated that harmony. His behaviour is a pretence, filling the scene with irony. Think about how the word 'play' in line 4 embodies that irony.

2 The Murderer's report (in pairs)

a The stage is set for a banquet, and there are many characters present. Macbeth is probably seated among his guests (line 10). So where and how does his conversation with the Murderer take place? Work out how the banquet might be staged (a diagram could be helpful) and how the characters could move. (For example, what is everyone else on stage doing whilst Macbeth talks with the Murderer?)

b Take parts and experiment with different ways of speaking lines 12–32. Does Macbeth whisper nervously, speak angrily, or does he pretend (to the watching thanes) that it's a normal conversation?

3 More euphemisms (see page 30)

'Dispatched', 'the like', 'it', 'safe' – once again Macbeth avoids naming the deed: murder. Read his lines to the Murderer, substituting (with great emphasis) 'kill' or 'murder' for Macbeth's evasive language.

---

degrees status or rank (which determined where they sat at table)
keeps her state stays on her throne
measure toast
the nonpareil without equal
fit anxiety

founded secure, immovable
As broad and general secure and free
casing surrounding
cribbed shut in a tiny space
saucy distressing

Act 3 Scene 4
The banqueting hall at Forres

Banquet prepared. Two thrones are placed on stage. Enter MACBETH
as King, LADY MACBETH *as Queen,* ROSS, LENNOX, LORDS, *and
attendants. Lady Macbeth sits*

MACBETH You know your own degrees, sit down; at first and last,
the hearty welcome.
> [*The Lords sit*]

LORDS Thanks to your majesty.

MACBETH Our self will mingle with society and play the humble
host; our hostess keeps her state, but in best time we will   5
require her welcome.

LADY MACBETH Pronounce it for me, sir, to all our friends, for
my heart speaks, they are welcome.

> *Enter* FIRST MURDERER

MACBETH See, they encounter thee with their hearts' thanks.
  Both sides are even; here I'll sit i'th'midst.   10
  Be large in mirth, anon we'll drink a measure
  The table round. [*To First Murderer*] There's blood upon
   thy face.

FIRST MURDERER 'Tis Banquo's then.

MACBETH 'Tis better thee without, than he within.
  Is he dispatched?   15

FIRST MURDERER My lord, his throat is cut; that I did for him.

MACBETH Thou art the best o'th'cut-throats,
  Yet he's good that did the like for Fleance;
  If thou didst it, thou art the nonpareil.

FIRST MURDERER Most royal sir, Fleance is scaped.   20

MACBETH Then comes my fit again: I had else been perfect;
  Whole as the marble, founded as the rock,
  As broad and general as the casing air:
  But now I am cabined, cribbed, confined, bound in
  To saucy doubts and fears. But Banquo's safe?   25

FIRST MURDERER Ay, my good lord: safe in a ditch he bides,
  With twenty trenchèd gashes on his head,
  The least a death to nature.

Macbeth consoles himself that Fleance is too young to do harm yet. Lady Macbeth bids him welcome his guests. The sight of Banquo's Ghost unnerves Macbeth. Lady Macbeth attempts to calm the Lords.

1 The Ghost of Banquo: seen or unseen? (in pairs)

Every time the play is produced, the director must decide whether or not to bring on a Ghost that the audience can see. Of all the characters on stage, only Macbeth sees the Ghost. In Shakespeare's time, and in the eighteenth and nineteenth centuries, the audience was shown the Ghost, but some modern productions leave the apparition to the audience's imagination.

Talk together about the advantages and disadvantages of an invisible Ghost. If you argue for having an actor play the Ghost, what does he look like, what does he wear and how does he move?

2 How does Macbeth behave?

Write notes to advise Macbeth how to deliver each of his speeches in lines 37–51. (Lines 40–1 mean 'if only Banquo were here, all the nobility of Scotland would be under our roof'.)

3 Ceremony (in pairs)

In lines 32–7 Lady Macbeth reminds Macbeth to welcome his guests ('give the cheer'), because without such welcoming toasts, it would be merely a paid-for meal ('sold'). Eating in company away from home should be enriched by such ceremony ('From thence, the sauce to meat is ceremony'). State banquets today still use elaborate ceremonies (toasts, speeches, and so on). Talk together about what you think 'ceremony' adds to people taking a meal together.

---

grown serpent Banquo
worm Fleance
give the cheer welcome your
 guests
is sold ... without it unless there are
 many ceremonious welcomes, it's like
 a take-away meal

Who may ... mischance I hope he's
 absent because of unkindness rather
 than an accident
gory locks blood-covered hair
much you note him you watch him
 closely
Are you a man? see page 161

MACBETH   Thanks for that.
There the grown serpent lies; the worm that's fled
Hath nature that in time will venom breed,   30
No teeth for th'present. Get thee gone; tomorrow
We'll hear ourselves again.
                              Exit [First] Murderer

LADY MACBETH   My royal lord,
You do not give the cheer; the feast is sold
That is not often vouched while 'tis a-making,
'Tis given with welcome. To feed were best at home: 35
From thence, the sauce to meat is ceremony,
Meeting were bare without it.

Enter the Ghost of Banquo and sits in Macbeth's place

MACBETH   Sweet remembrancer!
Now good digestion wait on appetite,
And health on both.

LENNOX   May't please your highness, sit.

MACBETH Here had we now our country's honour roofed,   40
Were the graced person of our Banquo present,
Who may I rather challenge for unkindness
Than pity for mischance.

ROSS   His absence, sir,
Lays blame upon his promise. Please't your highness
To grace us with your royal company?   45

MACBETH The table's full.

LENNOX   Here is a place reserved, sir.

MACBETH Where?

LENNOX Here, my good lord. What is't that moves your highness?

MACBETH Which of you have done this?

LORDS   What, my good lord?

MACBETH Thou canst not say I did it; never shake   50
Thy gory locks at me!

ROSS Gentlemen, rise, his highness is not well.
                [Lady Macbeth joins the Lords]

LADY MACBETH Sit, worthy friends. My lord is often thus,
And hath been from his youth. Pray you, keep seat.
The fit is momentary; upon a thought   55
He will again be well. If much you note him
You shall offend him and extend his passion.
Feed, and regard him not. *[To Macbeth]* Are you a man?

Lady Macbeth rebukes Macbeth for his display of fear. The Ghost leaves. Macbeth broods on how the dead return. He recovers his composure, reassures the thanes and proposes a toast. The Ghost re-enters.

1 Whispering (in pairs)

Much of lines 58–83 ('Are you . . . murder is') is an intensely private conversation (even though the startled thanes must be eager to listen to what is being said). No one must hear the incriminating words about the dagger, or Duncan, or murders. Sit close together and whisper the words to each other. Change characters and repeat. Work out how the audience would hear the conversation, but the banquet guests would not.

'Prithee, see there! Behold, look, lo!' Macbeth challenges the Ghost to speak, believing Banquo has returned from a charnel-house (storehouse for the bones of the dead). But Lady Macbeth and the guests can see only an empty chair. Write down several reasons why only Macbeth can see the Ghost. Compare your reasons with those of other students.

O proper stuff! rubbish!
flaws and starts sudden tantrums
Imposters to false in comparison with
grandam grandmother
charnel-houses stores of bones
monuments graves

maws of kites stomachs of birds of prey
Ere humane statute purged before law banished evil from
weal commonwealth
muse wonder
infirmity weakness

MACBETH Ay, and a bold one, that dare look on that
        Which might appal the devil.
LADY MACBETH   O proper stuff!   60
        This is the very painting of your fear;
        This is the air-drawn dagger which you said
        Led you to Duncan. O, these flaws and starts,
        Impostors to true fear, would well become
        A woman's story at a winter's fire   65
        Authorised by her grandam. Shame itself!
        Why do you make such faces? When all's done
        You look but on a stool.
MACBETH Prithee, see there! Behold, look, lo! How say you?
        [*To Ghost*] Why, what care I? If thou canst nod, speak too.   70
        If charnel-houses and our graves must send
        Those that we bury back, our monuments
        Shall be the maws of kites.
                        [*Exit Ghost of Banquo*]
LADY MACBETH   What, quite unmanned in folly?
MACBETH If I stand here, I saw him.
LADY MACBETH   Fie, for shame.
MACBETH Blood hath been shed ere now, i'th'olden time,   75
        Ere humane statute purged the gentle weal;
        Ay, and since too, murders have been performed
        Too terrible for the ear. The time has been
        That when the brains were out, the man would die,
        And there an end. But now they rise again   80
        With twenty mortal murders on their crowns
        And push us from our stools. This is more strange
        Than such a murder is.
LADY MACBETH   My worthy lord,
        Your noble friends do lack you.
MACBETH   I do forget –
        Do not muse at me, my most worthy friends.   85
        I have a strange infirmity which is nothing
        To those that know me. Come, love and health to all,
        Then I'll sit down. Give me some wine; fill full!

        Enter Ghost [of Banquo]

        I drink to th'general joy o'th'whole table,

Macbeth, his composure recovered, proposes a toast to Banquo and the guests. On seeing the Ghost again he bursts into violent language, commanding him away. Lady Macbeth orders the Lords to leave.

---

1 Second appearance (in pairs)

Work out how the Ghost enters and how he behaves during Macbeth's violent outbursts (lines 89–107).

2 Banishing a ghost (whole class – a noisy activity!)

To experience the power of Macbeth's language, divide the class in two. The two groups face each other across the room. Take lines 93–107 and, in turn, hurl a short section at each other:

> Group 1: Avaunt and quit my sight!
> Group 2: Let the earth hide thee!
> Group 1: Thy bones are marrowless, thy blood is cold.

Accompany your phrases with appropriate gestures.

3 'What sights, my lord?'

The guests at the banquet are amazed at Macbeth's strange behaviour. Ross asks a question: 'What sights, my lord?' that expresses the guests' suspicions – what is it that Macbeth is seeing? As director of the play, advise everyone present on stage at this moment just how they should behave (and why) as they hear Ross's question.

4 'Stand not upon the order of your going'

Lady Macbeth orders the guests to leave immediately without any thought of precedence or rank (usually the most senior would leave first). Turn back to line 1 of this scene and note the contrast between then and now.

Our . . . pledge   here's to our homage and the toast
speculation   sight
peers   lords, thanes
Hyrcan tiger   savage tiger (supposed to live in Hyrcania, near the Caspian Sea)

If trembling . . . girl   if I tremble, call me a girl
admired   wondered at
strange . . . owe   wonder if I really am courageous
ruby   redness
blanched   made pale

And to our dear friend Banquo, whom we miss.   90
Would he were here! To all, and him we thirst,
And all to all.

LORDS   Our duties and the pledge.

MACBETH Avaunt and quit my sight! Let the earth hide thee!
Thy bones are marrowless, thy blood is cold;
Thou hast no speculation in those eyes   95
Which thou dost glare with.

LADY MACBETH   Think of this, good peers,
But as a thing of custom. 'Tis no other,
Only it spoils the pleasure of the time.

MACBETH What man dare, I dare;
Approach thou like the rugged Russian bear,   100
The armed rhinoceros, or th'Hyrcan tiger,
Take any shape but that, and my firm nerves
Shall never tremble. Or be alive again,
And dare me to the desert with thy sword;
If trembling I inhabit then, protest me   105
The baby of a girl. Hence horrible shadow,
Unreal mock'ry hence.

                        [*Exit Ghost of Banquo*]
                    Why so, being gone,
I am a man again. – Pray you, sit still.

LADY MACBETH You have displaced the mirth, broke the good
        meeting
With most admired disorder.

MACBETH   Can such things be,   110
And overcome us like a summer's cloud,
Without our special wonder? You make me strange
Even to the disposition that I owe,
When now I think you can behold such sights
And keep the natural ruby of your cheeks,   115
When mine is blanched with fear.

ROSS   What sights, my lord?

LADY MACBETH I pray you speak not; he grows worse and worse.
Question enrages him. At once, good night.
Stand not upon the order of your going,
But go at once.

The Lords leave. Macbeth broods on murder and unnaturalness. He vows to visit the Witches to know his future, swearing that from now on there is no turning back. He will kill anyone standing in his way.

---

1 'Blood will have blood' (in pairs)

After the disturbed action of the banquet, the final episode of the scene is usually played slowly in a still and eerie atmosphere. Macbeth and his wife are left alone together. She seems exhausted, but he enters a mysterious personal world of evil, and finds a renewed energy in his determination to visit the Witches and to wipe out anyone who might oppose him.

Write how you would stage lines 122–44 to greatest dramatic effect. Work on some of the following activities to help your thinking.

a 'It will have blood . . .'. Lines 122–6 are like an incantation. It sounds like something spoken by the Witches. Take turns to speak the lines to bring out their spell-like nature.

b Pauses. Pausing in a speech, or between speeches, can add much to dramatic effect. Identify several points in the episode where you would advise Macbeth to pause to show the troubled movement of his thoughts.

c Lines 135–8 ('For mine own good . . .') show Macbeth's determination to do any action, however evil, to further his own interests. He imagines blood as a river in which he has waded so far he may as well continue. Do you think he speaks the lines to Lady Macbeth, to himself, or . . . ?

d Movement. Are the Macbeths seated throughout? What actions might they perform? How do they finally leave the stage? (Such decisions can help the audience understand the Macbeths' relationship at this point.)

Augures, and understood relations prophecies, and meaningful patterns
maggot-pies, and choughs magpies and birds like crows
denies his person / At absents himself from

a servant feed a paid spy
worst means most evil methods
acted . . . scanned done at once without thought
initiate inexperienced, first
wants hard use needs testing
young in deed beginners in crime

LENNOX   Good night, and better health   120
        Attend his majesty.
LADY MACBETH   A kind good night to all.
                          [*Exeunt*] *Lords* [*and Attendants*]
MACBETH It will have blood they say: blood will have blood.
        Stones have been known to move and trees to speak.
        Augures, and understood relations, have
        By maggot-pies, and choughs, and rooks brought forth   125
        The secret'st man of blood. What is the night?
LADY MACBETH Almost at odds with morning, which is which.
MACBETH How sayst thou that Macduff denies his person
        At our great bidding?
LADY MACBETH   Did you send to him, sir?
MACBETH I hear it by the way, but I will send.   130
        There's not a one of them but in his house
        I keep a servant feed. I will tomorrow –
        And betimes I will – to the weïrd sisters.
        More shall they speak. For now I am bent to know
        By the worst means, the worst; for mine own good,   135
        All causes shall give way. I am in blood
        Stepped in so far that should I wade no more,
        Returning were as tedious as go o'er.
        Strange things I have in head that will to hand,
        Which must be acted ere they may be scanned.   140
LADY MACBETH You lack the season of all natures, sleep.
MACBETH Come, we'll to sleep. My strange and self-abuse
        Is the initiate fear that wants hard use;
        We are yet but young in deed.
                                            Exeunt

Hecate rebukes the Witches for speaking to Macbeth without involving her. She bids them meet her at the pit of Acheron to tell Macbeth of his destiny. She promises to use magic to ruin the over-confident Macbeth.

---

1 Is it by Shakespeare? (in pairs)

Scene 5 links the previous scene in which Macbeth decides to visit the Witches with the opening of Act 4 when he meets them. But there have been many arguments about whether Shakespeare himself wrote the scene (or another playwright called Thomas Middleton, see page 100). Take parts and read it aloud, then change roles and read it again. Afterwards, talk together about whether you think it is by Shakespeare.

2 Stage the scene (in small groups)

This scene is often cut in stage performances. Imagine you have decided to include it. How will you stage it, and what will your Hecate look like? (Some critics think it was included to give an opportunity for spectacular effects, such as Hecate flying.)

3 Find the lines

Identify the sections in lines 2–35 that match the following parts of Hecate's meaning: (i) reasons for anger; (ii) self-centred Macbeth; (iii) meet tomorrow with spells; (iv) I'm off to collect moon-vapour for magic to ruin Macbeth; (v) Macbeth's future; (vi) My spirit calls.

4 'Security': a change of meaning

The meaning of 'security' (line 32) has changed. In Shakespeare's time it meant 'being over-confident' or 'lacking anxiety'. That seems to describe Macbeth at the end of the previous scene. He no longer worries that the evil deeds he intends will result in the damnation of his soul.

Hecate   goddess of witchcraft
beldams   hags
close contriver   secret maker
Acheron   a river in Hell
vap'rous drop profound   magical potion

sleights   tricks
artificial sprites   apparitions, false spirits
bear ... wisdom   have unwise and unrealistic ambitions
security   over-confidence

Act 3 Scene 5
A desolate place

Thunder. Enter the three WITCHES, meeting HECATE

FIRST WITCH Why how now, Hecate, you look angerly?
HECATE Have I not reason, beldams, as you are,
        Saucy and over-bold? How did you dare
        To trade and traffic with Macbeth
        In riddles and affairs of death?   5
        And I the mistress of your charms,
        The close contriver of all harms,
        Was never called to bear my part
        Or show the glory of our art?
        And which is worse, all you have done   10
        Hath been but for a wayward son,
        Spiteful and wrathful, who, as others do,
        Loves for his own ends, not for you.
        But make amends now. Get you gone,
        And at the pit of Acheron   15
        Meet me i'th'morning. Thither he
        Will come to know his destiny.
        Your vessels and your spells provide,
        Your charms and every thing beside.
        I am for th'air. This night I'll spend   20
        Unto a dismal and a fatal end.
        Great business must be wrought ere noon.
        Upon the corner of the moon
        There hangs a vap'rous drop profound;
        I'll catch it ere it come to ground;   25
        And that distilled by magic sleights,
        Shall raise such artificial sprites
        As by the strength of their illusion
        Shall draw him on to his confusion.
        He shall spurn fate, scorn death, and bear   30
        His hopes 'bove wisdom, grace, and fear.
        And you all know, security
        Is mortals' chiefest enemy.

Lennox comments guardedly and ironically on Macbeth's guilt as he recounts the killing of Duncan, Banquo and the grooms. He hints at Macbeth's murderous intentions towards Malcolm, Donaldbain and Fleance.

---

1 Language and tyranny (in pairs)

Under a dictatorship, everyone must watch their language. It's dangerous to voice your thoughts openly. Turn Lennox's lines 1–24 into a conversation by speaking small sections in turn. You'll find that it works well as a guarded and ironic conversation where both speakers are afraid to speak the truth plainly.

Afterwards, improvise a conversation between two citizens in a totalitarian state, testing each other to find if they are allies in the cause of freedom.

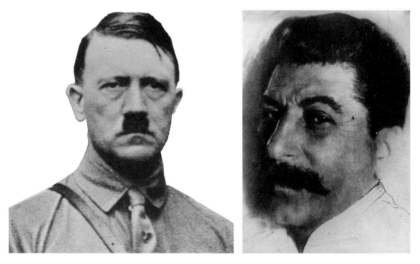

Hitler and Stalin were tyrants who, like Macbeth, ruled by fear, suppressing free speech and opposition. In Nazi Germany and the Communist Soviet Union, men and women had to be as guarded in their speech as Lennox. Spies and informers were always around to betray those who spoke openly.

---

but hit your thoughts   echoed your own beliefs
strangely borne   oddly carried out
marry   indeed (by St Mary)
too late   at night

want the thought   fail to think
thralls   prisoners
under his key   within his power
broad words   frank talk
bestows himself   lives now

Music, and a song[, 'Come away, come away', within]
    Hark, I am called: my little spirit, see,
    Sits in a foggy cloud, and stays for me.   *[Exit]*   35
FIRST WITCH Come, let's make haste; she'll soon be back again.
                                           Exeunt

Act 3 Scene 6
The castle of Lennox

Enter LENNOX and another LORD

LENNOX My former speeches have but hit your thoughts
    Which can interpret further; only I say
    Things have been strangely borne. The gracious Duncan
    Was pitied of Macbeth; marry, he was dead.
    And the right-valiant Banquo walked too late,   5
    Whom you may say, if't please you, Fleance killed,
    For Fleance fled. Men must not walk too late.
    Who cannot want the thought how monstrous
    It was for Malcolm and for Donaldbain
    To kill their gracious father? Damnèd fact,   10
    How it did grieve Macbeth! Did he not straight
    In pious rage the two delinquents tear,
    That were the slaves of drink and thralls of sleep?
    Was not that nobly done? Ay, and wisely too,
    For 'twould have angered any heart alive   15
    To hear the men deny't. So that I say,
    He has borne all things well, and I do think
    That had he Duncan's sons under his key –
    As, an't please heaven, he shall not – they should find
    What 'twere to kill a father. So should Fleance.   20
    But peace, for from broad words, and 'cause he failed
    His presence at the tyrant's feast, I hear
    Macduff lives in disgrace. Sir, can you tell
    Where he bestows himself?

The unnamed Lord tells of Malcolm's warm welcome in England, and of Macduff's plea to King Edward for an army to overthrow Macbeth's tyranny. He reports Macduff's refusal to visit Macbeth.

---

1 Who is the unnamed Lord?

The unnamed Lord has a similar dramatic function to the Old Man of Act 2 Scene 4, who represented the ordinary people of Scotland. His words are of hope and eventual peace. Do you think he should have a name, or remain as a representative voice, like a chorus?

2 'Our suffering country' (in groups of six or more)

Lines 34–6 describe all that is absent in Scotland under Macbeth's tyrannical rule. Identify the five elements in the lines and make five tableaux, each of which shows 'present Scotland' and 'future Scotland' (for example, starving in the present versus feasting in the future, sleeplessness versus tranquil sleep, and so on).

3 'The cloudy messenger'

In several of Shakespeare's plays, the messenger who brings bad news gets into trouble merely for reporting it. Macbeth's 'cloudy messenger' of lines 41–4 is obviously resentful of Macduff's refusal to return to Scotland. It will hinder ('clog') the messenger's career prospects.

Imagine you are the messenger travelling back to Macbeth with the bad news of Macduff's answer. Work out a story that tells the truth but that you hope will avoid your being punished by Macbeth.

4 Good and evil (in groups of three)

One person quietly reads aloud the whole scene. Another echoes every word to do with evil or wrongdoing (for example, 'strangely', 'deed'). The third person echoes every word to do with goodness, hope or Heaven (for example, 'gracious', 'right-valiant').

---

holds the due of birth steals his birthright, the crown
Edward King Edward the Confessor (reigned 1042–66)
with such grace . . . respect with full dignity, despite the loss of his throne
pray request
him above God
ratify justify
cloudy sullen
hums mutters
to a caution to be careful

LORD   The son of Duncan,
     From whom this tyrant holds the due of birth,   25
     Lives in the English court and is received
     Of the most pious Edward with such grace,
     That the malevolence of fortune nothing
     Takes from his high respect. Thither Macduff
     Is gone to pray the holy king upon his aid   30
     To wake Northumberland and warlike Siward,
     That by the help of these, with him above
     To ratify the work, we may again
     Give to our tables meat, sleep to our nights,
     Free from our feasts and banquets bloody knives,   35
     Do faithful homage and receive free honours,
     All which we pine for now. And this report
     Hath so exasperate their king that he
     Prepares for some attempt of war.

LENNOX Sent he to Macduff?   40

LORD He did. And with an absolute, 'Sir, not I',
     The cloudy messenger turns me his back
     And hums, as who should say, 'You'll rue the time
     That clogs me with this answer.'

LENNOX   And that well might
     Advise him to a caution t'hold what distance   45
     His wisdom can provide. Some holy angel
     Fly to the court of England and unfold
     His message ere he come, that a swift blessing
     May soon return to this our suffering country
     Under a hand accursed.

LORD   I'll send my prayers with him.   50

Exeunt

Looking back at Act 3
Activities for groups or individuals

1 The coronation of Macbeth

Act 3 opens shortly after Macbeth has been crowned at Scone as High King of Scotland. The coronation is not shown in the play.

Either invent a suitable coronation ceremony for the new king and queen. You will need words and actions of great ritual and formality to match the importance of the event.

Or write an account of the coronation as seen by a participant.

2 Things go wrong

In Scene 1 Macbeth plans to make his new status secure, proposing a council meeting and a banquet, and plotting Banquo's murder. Banquo is killed, but his son escapes, and in Scene 4 the banquet becomes a nightmare for Macbeth and arouses the suspicions of the guests. The act ends with signs of opposition: a planned invasion by Macduff and Malcolm.

Write six paragraphs, one for each scene, which show how Macbeth's kingship becomes less and less secure.

3 What happened?

The thanes are abruptly dismissed from the banquet in Scene 4. Step into role as a thane (invent your title) and write your recollection of what happened at the banquet.

4 Changing relationship

Act 3 is the last time the Macbeths are seen together. It also displays how their relationship has changed. Previously, Lady Macbeth had been the leader, prompting Macbeth to the murder of Duncan. Identify each time she appears in this act, and write several sentences describing how her relationship with her husband changes.

5 'Good things of day begin to droop and drowse'

One critic thought line 52 in Scene 2 was 'the motto of the entire tragedy'. Use the line to design a poster advertising a production.

Macbeth and Lady Macbeth have got what they wanted, but it has not brought them happiness. Macbeth is tortured by his conscience, and although Lady Macbeth tries to comfort him, she too is racked with anxiety. They have achieved their ambition, the crown, at great mental cost. Compare the picture above with how the Macbeths are portrayed in the colour illustrations and on other pages. Then look back through the act and identify lines which show the mental suffering the two characters endure.

6 Appearance versus reality

The theme of deceptive appearance runs all through Act 3. In each scene find a quotation which implies that appearance does not match reality.

The Witches' familiars have declared the time has come to meet Macbeth. Engrossed in their ugly ritual, they chant as they circle the cauldron, throwing in repulsive ingredients to make a sickening brew.

---

1 Act it out! (in groups of three or more)

Work out the most dramatic way to stage lines 1–38. You'll find that you can quickly learn the lines because of their rhythm and content. If you work in groups larger than three, share the lines or speak them together. Think about the atmosphere you wish to create: Horror? Evil? Danger?

2 An ecological view (in pairs)

Shakespeare's Witches regarded certain animals and reptiles as evil, associated with black magic and night-time. Today, many people regard them quite differently – not as evil, but as our fellow creatures on earth. One person reads lines 1–38. The other, as ecologist, interrupts after each animal or reptile is mentioned, to explain their 'good' aspects. Here are some explanations to help you (others are given at the foot of the page):

hedge-pig hedgehog
blind-worm slow-worm
howlet young owl
mummy mummified corpse
hemlock poisonous plant
yew poisonous tree

3 Invent your own recipe: hellish or divine

Make a hell-broth of your own by thinking up your own ingredients. Use the same rhythms as the Witches. What difference does it make if you invent a 'divine-stew' with pleasant ingredients?

---

brindled streaked with colour
Harpier name of a familiar (a harpy had a woman's face and a bird's body); lines 1–3 are about the Witches' familiars (see page 2)
Sweltered venom poisonous sweat
fenny slimy

maw and gulf stomach and throat
ravined full of devoured prey
Jew . . . Turk . . . Tartar all non-Christians
drab prostitute
slab sticky
chawdron entrails, stomach

Act 4 Scene 1
A desolate place near Forres

Thunder. Enter the three WITCHES [with a cauldron]

FIRST WITCH Thrice the brindled cat hath mewed.
SECOND WITCH Thrice and once the hedge-pig whined.
THIRD WITCH Harpier cries, ''Tis time, 'tis time.'
FIRST WITCH Round about the cauldron go;
    In the poisoned entrails throw. 5
    Toad, that under cold stone
    Days and nights has thirty-one
    Sweltered venom sleeping got,
    Boil thou first i'th'charmèd pot.
ALL Double, double toil and trouble; 10
    Fire burn, and cauldron bubble.
SECOND WITCH Fillet of a fenny snake,
    In the cauldron boil and bake:
    Eye of newt, and toe of frog,
    Wool of bat, and tongue of dog, 15
    Adder's fork, and blind-worm's sting,
    Lizard's leg, and howlet's wing,
    For a charm of powerful trouble,
    Like a hell-broth, boil and bubble.
ALL Double, double toil and trouble, 20
    Fire burn, and cauldron bubble.
THIRD WITCH Scale of dragon, tooth of wolf,
    Witches' mummy, maw and gulf
    Of the ravined salt-sea shark,
    Root of hemlock, digged i'th'dark; 25
    Liver of blaspheming Jew,
    Gall of goat, and slips of yew,
    Slivered in the moon's eclipse;
    Nose of Turk, and Tartar's lips,
    Finger of birth-strangled babe, 30
    Ditch-delivered by a drab,
    Make the gruel thick and slab.
    Add thereto a tiger's chawdron
    For th'ingredience of our cauldron.

The Witches complete the preparation of their hellish brew and are congratulated by Hecate. Macbeth enters and challenges them to answer what he asks, irrespective of the most appalling consequences.

1 Hecate and 'Black spirits'

The words of the song appear in *The Witches*, a play by Thomas Middleton (a contemporary of Shakespeare). Hecate's lines are usually cut in modern productions of the play (perhaps because the image of 'elves and fairies' is too tame). Would you include Hecate's lines if you were directing the play? Give reasons for your decision.

2 Tell me – though destruction follows (in small groups)

Macbeth is obsessed with one thought: the desire to know the future. He appeals to the Witches to answer him, even if the result is the destruction of the world. His language is like that of the Witches: 'I conjure you' is the beginning of a spell or incantation. Try one or more of these activities on lines 49–60:

a One person whispers the lines; the others echo every 'though'.

b Everyone speaks the lines together as a witch-like spell.

c Share them out and add appropriate sound effects.

d Compare them with *King Lear* Act 3 Scene 2, lines 1–9.

3 'Though bladed corn be lodged' (line 54)

Witches were believed to have the power to move corn from place to place, or to flatten it. That superstition still lingers. 'Corn circles' (corn flattened into intricate shapes) still often appear in England and the USA. Though many people believe that corn circles are an elaborate hoax, many others believe that they are supernatural, the work of extra-terrestrial beings.

---

yeasty frothy
navigation shipping
bladed . . . lodged growing corn is flattened

warders owners, keepers
slope bend
nature's germen the seeds of all life

ALL Double, double toil and trouble,   35
       Fire burn, and cauldron bubble.
SECOND WITCH Cool it with a baboon's blood,
       Then the charm is firm and good.

    Enter HECATE, *and the other three Witches*

HECATE O well done! I commend your pains,
       And every one shall share i'th'gains;   40
       And now about the cauldron sing
       Like elves and fairies in a ring,
       Enchanting all that you put in.
       Music, and a song, 'Black spirits, etc.'
       [Exeunt Hecate and the other three Witches]
SECOND WITCH By the pricking of my thumbs,
       Something wicked this way comes;   45
       Open locks, whoever knocks.

    Enter MACBETH

MACBETH How now, you secret, black, and midnight hags!
       What is't you do?
ALL THE WITCHES   A deed without a name.
MACBETH I conjure you by that which you profess,
       Howe'er you come to know it, answer me.   50
       Though you untie the winds and let them fight
       Against the churches, though the yeasty waves
       Confound and swallow navigation up,
       Though bladed corn be lodged and trees blown down,
       Though castles topple on their warders' heads,   55
       Though palaces and pyramids do slope
       Their heads to their foundations, though the treasure
       Of nature's germen tumble altogether
       Even till destruction sicken: answer me
       To what I ask you.
FIRST WITCH   Speak.
SECOND WITCH   Demand.
THIRD WITCH   We'll answer.   60
FIRST WITCH Say, if thou'dst rather hear it from our mouths,
       Or from our masters'?
MACBETH   Call 'em, let me see 'em.

The Witches show their Apparitions. An armed Head warns Macbeth: 'beware Macduff'. A bloody Child tells him that no naturally born man can harm him. Macbeth, though reassured, swears to kill Macduff.

The Witches prepare to show Macbeth the Apparitions.

1 Show the Apparitions (in small groups)

Rehearse a presentation of lines 60–93. The three Apparitions are invitations to exercise your imagination. Talk together about what each might symbolise: for example, 'an armed Head' might forecast Macbeth's eventual fate at the hands of Macduff, 'a bloody Child' the death of Macduff's children, and 'a Child crowned, with a tree in his hand' Malcolm's victory. In Shakespeare's theatre they probably appeared through a trapdoor. Stage your own entrances however you think best.

---

farrow   litter of piglets
the murderer's gibbet   where a
  murderer was hanged
office   function, purpose
deftly   skilfully
harped   echoed
potent   powerful

assurance double sure   my security
  even more sure
take a bond of fate   swear a
  binding oath
issue   descendant, child
**the round / And top of
  sovereignty**   the crown

FIRST WITCH Pour in sow's blood, that hath eaten
    Her nine farrow; grease that's sweaten
    From the murderer's gibbet throw   65
    Into the flame.
ALL THE WITCHES   Come high or low:
    Thyself and office deftly show.

    Thunder. [*Enter*] FIRST APPARITION, *an armed Head*

MACBETH Tell me, thou unknown power –
FIRST WITCH   He knows thy thought;
    Hear his speech, but say thou nought.
FIRST APPARITION Macbeth, Macbeth, Macbeth: beware
    Macduff,   70
    Beware the Thane of Fife. Dismiss me. Enough.   *Descends*
MACBETH Whate'er thou art, for thy good caution, thanks;
    Thou hast harped my fear aright. But one word more –
FIRST WITCH He will not be commanded. Here's another,
    More potent than the first.   75

    Thunder. [*Enter*] SECOND APPARITION, *a bloody Child*

SECOND APPARITION Macbeth, Macbeth, Macbeth.
MACBETH Had I three ears, I'd hear thee.
SECOND APPARITION Be bloody, bold, and resolute; laugh to
    scorn
    The power of man, for none of woman born
    Shall harm Macbeth.   *Descends*   80
MACBETH Then live, Macduff, what need I fear of thee?
    But yet I'll make assurance double sure
    And take a bond of fate: thou shalt not live,
    That I may tell pale-hearted fear it lies,
    And sleep in spite of thunder.

  Thunder. [*Enter*] THIRD APPARITION, *a Child crowned, with a tree*
             in his hand

                  What is this,   85
    That rises like the issue of a king
    And wears upon his baby-brow the round
    And top of sovereignty?
ALL THE WITCHES   Listen, but speak not to't.

The Third Apparition promises that Macbeth will not be defeated until Birnam Wood comes to Dunsinane. Macbeth demands to know more about the future. The Witches present a procession of eight kings and Banquo.

1 A show of eight kings

Many believe that Shakespeare had King James I very much in mind as he wrote the play (see page 163). The eight kings are supposed to represent the ancestors of James. He saw *Macbeth* shortly after it was written. One story is that the eighth king carried a mirror ('glass') and, at lines 118–19, focused it on the watching King James, who therefore saw his own reflection and heard the promise that his descendants ('many more') would rule England.

The 'two-fold balls and treble sceptres' could also be a flattering reference to King James. They represent the two orbs he carried at his two coronations in Scotland and England, and the three kingdoms he now ruled: Scotland, England and Ireland.

Work in large groups to present your own version of what Macbeth sees. As one person speaks lines 111–23, your audience should see appropriate images of the kings and Banquo.

An eighteenth-century version of a show of eight kings.

lion-mettled courageous	**mortal custom** usual life-span
Who chafes . . . frets . . .	**sear** burn
conspirers rebels, dissidents	**th'crack of doom** doomsday, the
impress conscript	thunder of the Day of Judgement
bodements prophecies	**blood-boltered** spattered in blood
the lease of nature the length of	
natural life	

THIRD APPARITION Be lion-mettled, proud, and take no care
            Who chafes, who frets, or where conspirers are.   90
            Macbeth shall never vanquished be until
            Great Birnam Wood to high Dunsinane hill
            Shall come against him.   *Descends*
MACBETH   That will never be:
            Who can impress the forest, bid the tree
            Unfix his earthbound root? Sweet bodements, good.   95
            Rebellious dead, rise never till the wood
            Of Birnam rise, and our high-placed Macbeth
            Shall live the lease of nature, pay his breath
            To time and mortal custom. Yet my heart
            Throbs to know one thing. Tell me, if your art   100
            Can tell so much, shall Banquo's issue ever
            Reign in this kingdom?
ALL THE WITCHES   Seek to know no more.
MACBETH I will be satisfied. Deny me this,
            And an eternal curse fall on you. Let me know.
                 [Cauldron descends.] Hautboys
            Why sinks that cauldron? And what noise is this?   105
FIRST WITCH Show!
SECOND WITCH Show!
THIRD WITCH Show!
ALL THE WITCHES Show his eyes and grieve his heart,
            Come like shadows, so depart.   110
    [Enter] a show of eight kings, and [the] last with a glass in his hand[;
                 Banquo's Ghost following]
MACBETH Thou art too like the spirit of Banquo. Down!
            Thy crown does sear mine eyeballs. And thy hair,
            Thou other gold-bound brow, is like the first;
            A third, is like the former. – Filthy hags,
            Why do you show me this? – A fourth? Start, eyes!   115
            What, will the line stretch out to th'crack of doom?
            Another yet? A seventh? I'll see no more.
            And yet the eighth appears, who bears a glass
            Which shows me many more. And some I see,
            That two-fold balls and treble sceptres carry.   120
            Horrible sight! Now I see 'tis true,
            For the blood-boltered Banquo smiles upon me,
            And points at them for his.
                [Exeunt show of kings and Banquo's Ghost]
                What, is this so?

Having presented Banquo's descendants as kings, the Witches dance, then vanish, to Macbeth's anger. Hearing of Macduff's flight, Macbeth resolves to kill every member of Macduff's family he can catch.

---

1 Getting the Witches off the stage (in small groups)

Lines 124–31 are thought to have been written by Thomas Middleton, and are often cut in production. But many critics argue that the final two lines (130–1) represent another example of Shakespeare flattering King James, and were probably spoken directly to him at a performance in 1606. But whether or not that is true, every new production faces the practical problem of how the Witches leave the stage.

Work on the stage direction at line 131. Create a suitable dance sequence ('antic round', line 129) for the Witches which enables them to 'vanish' as dramatically as possible.

2 'Dread exploits' (in pairs)

In his soliloquy, Macbeth feels a great sense of urgency, as if he is in a battle with Time. He decides that purposes without action are useless, and resolves simply to follow his first instincts. The depth of brutality to which he has now sunk is revealed in his determination to massacre innocent women and children in Macduff's castle. Speak lines 143–54 ('Time . . . sights') as:

- private, whispered thoughts
- a party political broadcast to a huge audience
- the words of a very fearful man
- the words of an angry tyrant.

Afterwards, talk together about how the lines might be spoken in a stage performance, and what they add to your view of Macbeth.

---

antic round mad dance
aye accursèd cursed for ever
flighty purpose flying thoughts, first intentions
never is o'ertook never happens

The very firstlings . . . hand I'll act on my first instincts
give . . . o'th'sword kill
trace him in his line descend from him

FIRST WITCH Ay, sir, all this is so. But why
               Stands Macbeth thus amazedly? 125
               Come, sisters, cheer we up his sprites,
               And show the best of our delights.
               I'll charm the air to give a sound,
               While you perform your antic round
               That this great king may kindly say, 130
               Our duties did his welcome pay.
            Music. The Witches dance, and vanish
MACBETH Where are they? Gone? Let this pernicious hour,
               Stand aye accursèd in the calendar.
               Come in, without there!

               Enter LENNOX

LENNOX   What's your grace's will?
MACBETH Saw you the weïrd sisters?
LENNOX   No, my lord. 135
MACBETH Came they not by you?
LENNOX   No indeed, my lord.
MACBETH Infected be the air whereon they ride,
               And damned all those that trust them. I did hear
               The galloping of horse. Who was't came by?
LENNOX 'Tis two or three, my lord, that bring you word 140
               Macduff is fled to England.
MACBETH   Fled to England?
LENNOX Ay, my good lord.
MACBETH [*Aside*] Time, thou anticipat'st my dread exploits;
               The flighty purpose never is o'ertook
               Unless the deed go with it. From this moment, 145
               The very firstlings of my heart shall be
               The firstlings of my hand. And even now
               To crown my thoughts with acts, be it thought and done.
               The castle of Macduff I will surprise;
               Seize upon Fife; give to th'edge o'th'sword 150
               His wife, his babes, and all unfortunate souls
               That trace him in his line. No boasting like a fool;
               This deed I'll do before this purpose cool,
               But no more sights. – Where are these gentlemen?
               Come, bring me where they are. 155
                          Exeunt

Macduff's wife interprets his flight to England as madness, fear, or lack of love for his family. Ross comforts her: Macduff knows best, and even though the times are dangerous, they will improve.

---

1 Scene change (in pairs)

Shakespeare's stagecraft is evident in the immediate scene change. From Macbeth's violent thoughts after meeting the Witches, the action shifts to Macduff's castle and the innocence of Macduff's wife and child. How would you perform the scene change? Make your suggestions, ensuring that the action will flow swiftly.

2 Seeds of hope? (in small groups)

Ross talks of how the cruelty of Macbeth's tyranny has affected people's integrity. Men can be traitors without even knowing it themselves (lines 18–19); fears breed rumours (lines 19–20); and everyone is adrift in an unpredictable world (lines 21–2). But he thinks the tide will turn: evil will give way to good (lines 24–5).

Do you think his words reassure Lady Macduff? Talk together about whether you agree with Ross's view that bad always gives way to good.

3 Crocodile tears? (in pairs)

Ross leaves, near to tears. In Roman Polanski's 1971 film of the play, Ross is an obvious hypocrite, a time-server. He puts on a friendly face to ensure that he can keep in with whoever is in power. As he leaves Macduff's castle, he waves the Murderers in to kill everyone inside. Playing Ross in that way adds to the sense of Scotland's corruption.

How do you see Ross? Look back through all he has said so far and talk together about whether or not you think him sincere.

---

titles possessions
wants the natural touch lacks feeling
  for his family
diminutive tiny
All is the fear . . . love he's filled with
  fear, not love

coz cousin
school control
The fits o'th'season the violence of
  the times
I am so much . . . discomfort
  (I'm likely to weep if I stay)

Act 4 Scene 2
Fife The castle of Macduff

Enter LADY MACDUFF, *her* SON, *and* ROSS

LADY MACDUFF What had he done, to make him fly the land?
ROSS You must have patience, madam.
LADY MACDUFF   He had none;
    His flight was madness. When our actions do not,
    Our fears do make us traitors.
ROSS   You know not
    Whether it was his wisdom or his fear.   5
LADY MACDUFF Wisdom? To leave his wife, to leave his babes,
    His mansion, and his titles in a place
    From whence himself does fly? He loves us not.
    He wants the natural touch, for the poor wren,
    The most diminutive of birds, will fight,   10
    Her young ones in her nest, against the owl.
    All is the fear, and nothing is the love;
    As little is the wisdom, where the flight
    So runs against all reason.
ROSS   My dearest coz,
    I pray you school yourself. But for your husband,   15
    He is noble, wise, judicious, and best knows
    The fits o'th'season. I dare not speak much further,
    But cruel are the times when we are traitors
    And do not know ourselves, when we hold rumour
    From what we fear, yet know not what we fear,   20
    But float upon a wild and violent sea,
    Each way and none. I take my leave of you;
    Shall not be long but I'll be here again.
    Things at the worst will cease, or else climb upward
    To what they were before. My pretty cousin,   25
    Blessing upon you.
LADY MACDUFF Fathered he is, and yet he's fatherless.
ROSS I am so much a fool, should I stay longer
    It would be my disgrace and your discomfort.
    I take my leave at once.   *Exit*

Macduff's son teases his mother affectionately. Behind his playful words are glimpses of the dangerous times: traps for the innocent, and widespread treachery. A messenger arrives to warn of danger.

Lady Macduff and her children. Suggest several ways in which this image conveys the innocence and vulnerability that Macbeth is determined to destroy.

Sirrah affectionate use of 'sir'
lime/pitfall/gin methods of catching birds: a glue-like paste smeared on trees / a pit / a trap to catch a bird by the head or legs

swears promises to tell the truth
prattler chatterbox
in your state . . . perfect I have only good intentions towards you

LADY MACDUFF   Sirrah, your father's dead,   30
     And what will you do now? How will you live?
SON As birds do, mother.
LADY MACDUFF   What, with worms and flies?
SON With what I get I mean, and so do they.
LADY MACDUFF Poor bird, thou'dst never fear the net, nor lime,
     the pitfall, nor the gin.   35
SON Why should I, mother? Poor birds they are not set for.
          My father is not dead for all your saying.
LADY MACDUFF Yes, he is dead. How wilt thou do for a father?
SON Nay, how will you do for a husband?
LADY MACDUFF Why, I can buy me twenty at any market.   40
SON Then you'll buy 'em to sell again.
LADY MACDUFF Thou speak'st with all thy wit, and yet i'faith
     with wit enough for thee.
SON Was my father a traitor, mother?
LADY MACDUFF Ay, that he was.   45
SON What is a traitor?
LADY MACDUFF Why, one that swears and lies.
SON And be all traitors, that do so?
LADY MACDUFF Every one that does so is a traitor and must be
     hanged.   50
SON And must they all be hanged that swear and lie?
LADY MACDUFF Every one.
SON Who must hang them?
LADY MACDUFF Why, the honest men.
SON Then the liars and swearers are fools, for there are liars and   55
     swearers enough to beat the honest men and hang up them.
LADY MACDUFF Now God help thee, poor monkey, but how wilt
     thou do for a father?
SON If he were dead, you'd weep for him; if you would not, it were
     a good sign that I should quickly have a new father.   60
LADY MACDUFF Poor prattler, how thou talk'st!

Enter a MESSENGER

MESSENGER Bless you, fair dame. I am not to you known,
          Though in your state of honour I am perfect;
          I doubt some danger does approach you nearly.

The messenger warns Lady Macduff to flee with her children because terrible danger is near. The Murderers enter, seeking Macduff. They kill his son and pursue Macduff's wife to murder her off stage.

---

1 Who is the Messenger? (in pairs)

Despite Macbeth's reign of terror, some glimmers of goodness still flicker in Scotland. The Messenger is willing to risk his life to warn the Macduffs. Every production must decide whether to present the Messenger as an unknown person or someone who has already appeared in the play. In one production it was Macbeth himself, which heightened the sense of his cruelty and removed the goodness from the episode.

Talk together about the possible identity of the Messenger. Then write his or her story, which explains the warning visit to Lady Macduff.

2 Willing murderers (in small groups)

Once again, Macbeth has someone doing his dirty work for him. What kind of people are willing to undertake such dreadful business as murdering innocent women and children? What kind of society produces such callous killers? Talk together about what makes men willing to commit such appalling brutality – both in Macbeth's and in today's world.

3 On stage / off stage

In Greek tragedy, all killings take place off stage. The audience did not see the act of violence, but heard it reported later. Shakespeare devotes very few lines to the murders, but productions vary greatly in their presentation, often showing Lady Macduff killed on stage. Write how you would stage the final few lines, giving reasons for your decisions.

---

homely friendly
fell cruelty deadly danger
Which is ... person which is close
  at hand
laudable praiseworthy

unsanctified unholy
fry young fish (notice how images of
  fertility are used as terms of abuse:
  'egg' and 'fry')

If you will take a homely man's advice,   65
Be not found here. Hence with your little ones.
To fright you thus, methinks I am too savage;
To do worse to you were fell cruelty,
Which is too nigh your person. Heaven preserve you,
I dare abide no longer.   *Exit*
LADY MACDUFF   Whither should I fly?   70
I have done no harm. But I remember now
I am in this earthly world where to do harm
Is often laudable, to do good sometime
Accounted dangerous folly. Why then, alas,
Do I put up that womanly defence,   75
To say I have done no harm?

                    Enter MURDERERS

                                    What are these faces?
A MURDERER Where is your husband?
LADY MACDUFF I hope in no place so unsanctified,
    Where such as thou mayst find him.
A MURDERER   He's a traitor.
SON Thou liest, thou shag-haired villain.
A MURDERER   What, you egg!   80
    Young fry of treachery!
                    [*Kills him*]
SON   He has killed me, mother,
    Run away, I pray you!
                    Exit [*Lady Macduff*] *crying 'Murder'[, pursued by*
                              Murderers with her Son]

Macduff urges Malcolm to go to the defence of Scotland, which is suffering under Macbeth's tyranny. Malcolm voices his suspicions that Macduff is Macbeth's agent and has good reasons to betray him to Macbeth.

---

1 England: design the scene (in pairs)

Work out a simple but effective way of showing the audience that this scene takes place in England at the palace of King Edward.

2 Malcolm's suspicions about Macduff

Malcolm builds a strong case for his mistrust of Macduff:

- He is not sure that Macduff is telling the truth (line 11).
- Macbeth was once thought to be honest (lines 12–13).
- Macduff was a friend of Macbeth (line 13).
- Macbeth has left Macduff unharmed (line 14).
- Macduff may betray Malcolm to Macbeth (lines 14–15).
- Macduff may kill Malcolm for Macbeth (lines 16–17).
- Macbeth is a traitor (line 18).
- Even a good man may obey a wicked king (lines 19–20).
- Evil often tries to look like good (lines 21–3).
- Macduff has abruptly left his family behind in danger (lines 26–8).
- Malcolm has cause to be suspicious for his own safety (lines 29–30).

Imagine you are Macduff. Answer each of Malcolm's suspicions.

3 Religious echoes (in pairs)

There is a religious image in each of the three longer speeches opposite. Identify them, then talk together about how each of them could apply to Macbeth himself.

---

desolate shade   remote place
mortal   deadly
Bestride our downfall birthdom
 defend our suffering birthplace
Like syllable of dolour   similar cry
 of grief
redress   make better
discern of   be rewarded by

recoil / In an imperial charge   serve a
 royal command
transpose   change
the brightest   Lucifer (who fell from
 God's grace)
the brows of grace   the look of
 goodness

Act 4 Scene 3
England The palace of King Edward

Enter MALCOLM *and* MACDUFF

MALCOLM Let us seek out some desolate shade and there
    Weep our sad bosoms empty.

MACDUFF   Let us rather
    Hold fast the mortal sword and like good men
    Bestride our downfall birthdom; each new morn,
    New widows howl, new orphans cry, new sorrows   5
    Strike heaven on the face, that it resounds
    As if it felt with Scotland and yelled out
    Like syllable of dolour.

MALCOLM   What I believe, I'll wail;
    What know, believe; and what I can redress,
    As I shall find the time to friend, I will.   10
    What you have spoke, it may be so perchance.
    This tyrant, whose sole name blisters our tongues,
    Was once thought honest; you have loved him well –
    He hath not touched you yet. I am young, but something
    You may discern of him through me, and wisdom   15
    To offer up a weak, poor, innocent lamb
    T'appease an angry god.

MACDUFF I am not treacherous.

MALCOLM   But Macbeth is.
    A good and virtuous nature may recoil
    In an imperial charge. But I shall crave your pardon: 20
    That which you are, my thoughts cannot transpose;
    Angels are bright still, though the brightest fell.
    Though all things foul would wear the brows of grace,
    Yet grace must still look so.

MACDUFF   I have lost my hopes.

MALCOLM Perchance even there where I did find my doubts.   25
    Why in that rawness left you wife and child,
    Those precious motives, those strong knots of love,
    Without leave-taking? I pray you,

Malcolm's suspicions dismay Macduff. Malcolm tells him that he has English troops to support his cause, but that his own vices are far worse than Macbeth's.

1 Suspect every visitor

Malcolm is testing Macduff's sincerity. The terror of Macbeth's regime has made him suspect all visitors; after all, they may be Macbeth's secret agents. He now embarks on a strange way of testing Macduff's honesty, claiming that his own vices far exceed Macbeth's. Identify the line opposite where Malcolm embarks on this bizarre strategy, and suggest how he speaks, behaves and looks at this moment.

A historical parallel shows that Malcolm has good reason for his suspicion of visitors. Leon Trotsky (right) was Stalin's friend and ally in the Russian Revolution of 1917, but he fled Russia to escape Stalin's tyranny. One of Stalin's agents tricked his way into Trotsky's confidence in his safe haven in Mexico, then assassinated him with an ice-pick. Tyrants never forgive or forget.

jealousies suspicions	**withal** besides
lay thou thy basis sure rest secure	**hands uplifted in my right** soldiers
affeered confirmed (that is to say,	supporting me
Macbeth is securely king)	**grafted** rooted, ingrained
to boot as well	**be opened** come to flower
the yoke slavery	**confineless harms** limitless evils

Let not my jealousies be your dishonours,
But mine own safeties; you may be rightly just,   30
Whatever I shall think.

MACDUFF   Bleed, bleed, poor country.
Great tyranny, lay thou thy basis sure,
For goodness dare not check thee; wear thou thy wrongs,
The title is affeered. Fare thee well, lord,
I would not be the villain that thou think'st   35
For the whole space that's in the tyrant's grasp,
And the rich East to boot.

MALCOLM   Be not offended.
I speak not as in absolute fear of you:
I think our country sinks beneath the yoke;
It weeps, it bleeds, and each new day a gash   40
Is added to her wounds. I think withal
There would be hands uplifted in my right,
And here from gracious England have I offer
Of goodly thousands. But for all this,
When I shall tread upon the tyrant's head,   45
Or wear it on my sword, yet my poor country
Shall have more vices than it had before,
More suffer, and more sundry ways than ever,
By him that shall succeed.

MACDUFF   What should he be?

MALCOLM It is myself I mean – in whom I know   50
All the particulars of vice so grafted
That when they shall be opened, black Macbeth
Will seem as pure as snow, and the poor state
Esteem him as a lamb, being compared
With my confineless harms.

MACDUFF   Not in the legions   55
Of horrid hell can come a devil more damned
In evils to top Macbeth.

Malcolm lists Macbeth's vices, but claims that his own sexual desire is limitless, and he is infinitely greedy. Macduff finds reasons to excuse Malcolm's ungovernable lust and avarice.

1 Show Macbeth's evil (in large groups)

Malcolm begins by naming eight of Macbeth's evils. He is 'bloody' (murderous), 'luxurious' (lecherous), 'avaricious' (greedy), 'false', 'deceitful', 'sudden' (violent), 'malicious', and possesses 'every sin that has a name' (the seven deadly sins).

Work out a sequence of tableaux or short mimes to show Macbeth's nature. Each scene will show a quality listed in lines 57–60. Add a commentary to your presentation if you wish.

2 A man's view of women (in small groups)

Macduff doesn't find a problem with Malcolm's claim that he is infinitely lecherous. 'We have willing dames enough', he says, claiming that there will be more women than even Malcolm can cope with who will be willing to prostitute themselves to a king ('to greatness dedicate themselves').

Talk together about Macduff's dismissal of lust as an unimportant quality in a leader. Is that the kind of thing only a man could say? Is a leader's promiscuity of no relevance? Use examples of the much-publicised sexual activities of modern politicians as evidence in your arguments.

3 Greed – now that's more serious! (in small groups)

Greed is more serious than excessive sexual appetite, says Macduff (lines 84–7). But even that doesn't count against a king! Malcolm may fill his pockets with Scotland's wealth. Discuss what you think of Macduff's reasoning, and what it suggests about his character.

---

voluptuousness lust
continent impediments restraints
Boundless intemperance limitless lust
Convey your pleasures have sex
hoodwink deceive
ill-composed affection wicked emotions

stanchless avarice unquenchable greed
summer-seeming not long lasting
foisons abundance
your mere own simply of your own
portable bearable

MALCOLM   I grant him bloody,
        Luxurious, avaricious, false, deceitful,
        Sudden, malicious, smacking of every sin
        That has a name. But there's no bottom, none,   60
        In my voluptuousness: your wives, your daughters,
        Your matrons, and your maids could not fill up
        The cistern of my lust, and my desire
        All continent impediments would o'erbear
        That did oppose my will. Better Macbeth,   65
        Than such an one to reign.
MACDUFF   Boundless intemperance
        In nature is a tyranny; it hath been
        Th'untimely emptying of the happy throne
        And fall of many kings. But fear not yet
        To take upon you what is yours: you may   70
        Convey your pleasures in a spacious plenty
        And yet seem cold. The time you may so hoodwink.
        We have willing dames enough; there cannot be
        That vulture in you to devour so many
        As will to greatness dedicate themselves,   75
        Finding it so inclined.
MALCOLM   With this, there grows
        In my most ill-composed affection such
        A stanchless avarice that, were I king,
        I should cut off the nobles for their lands,
        Desire his jewels, and this other's house,   80
        And my more-having would be as a sauce
        To make me hunger more, that I should forge
        Quarrels unjust against the good and loyal,
        Destroying them for wealth.
MACDUFF   This avarice
        Sticks deeper, grows with more pernicious root   85
        Than summer-seeming lust, and it hath been
        The sword of our slain kings; yet do not fear,
        Scotland hath foisons to fill up your will
        Of your mere own. All these are portable,
        With other graces weighed.   90

Malcolm claims that he has no good qualities whatsoever, and seeks only to create chaos. Macduff condemns Malcolm as unfit to rule. Malcolm says that Macduff's reaction has removed his suspicions. He denies all vices.

---

1 The good king (in large groups)

In lines 92–4 Malcolm lists twelve qualities that a good king should possess: 'justice' (fairness), 'verity' (truthfulness), 'temp'rance' (self-control), 'stableness' (even-temperedness), 'bounty' (generosity), 'perseverance' (endurance), 'mercy' (forgiveness), 'lowliness' (humility), 'devotion' (piety), 'patience', 'courage', 'fortitude' (strength).

Work out a way of showing these 'king-becoming graces' (for example, by a sequence of tableaux or mimes).

2 Who's who? (in pairs)

Macduff can tolerate no more of Malcolm's self-condemnation, and rejects him as unfit to live. Macduff's impassioned outburst in lines 102–14 includes references to Malcolm, Macbeth, Duncan, Duncan's wife, Scotland and Macduff himself. As one person reads a line at a time, the other identifies aloud to whom (or what) Macduff is referring (for example, in line 102 it is 'Malcolm', in line 103 'Malcolm' and 'Scotland').

3 What is Malcolm really like?

Macduff's outburst finally convinces Malcolm that Macduff is sincere. In lines 125–31, Malcolm says what he is really like. Make a list of the qualities he describes (the punctuation will help you). Compare your list with the qualities of kingship in lines 92–4. What qualities has Malcolm not mentioned? From your experience of him in this scene, write another list giving your own view of his character.

---

division variety
concord peace
truest issue legitimate heir (Malcolm)
interdiction condemnation
blaspheme his breed slander his family
upon her knees praying

scruples suspicions
trains tricks
modest wisdom . . . haste common sense saved me
detraction accusations
abjure reject
forsworn untruthful

MALCOLM But I have none. The king-becoming graces –
　　　　As justice, verity, temp'rance, stableness,
　　　　Bounty, perseverance, mercy, lowliness,
　　　　Devotion, patience, courage, fortitude –
　　　　I have no relish of them, but abound　　　　　　95
　　　　In the division of each several crime,
　　　　Acting it many ways. Nay, had I power, I should
　　　　Pour the sweet milk of concord into hell,
　　　　Uproar the universal peace, confound
　　　　All unity on earth.
MACDUFF　　　　　　　O Scotland, Scotland!　　100
MALCOLM If such a one be fit to govern, speak.
　　　　I am as I have spoken.
MACDUFF　　　　　　　　Fit to govern?
　　　　No, not to live. O nation miserable!
　　　　With an untitled tyrant, bloody-sceptred,
　　　　When shalt thou see thy wholesome days again,　　105
　　　　Since that the truest issue of thy throne
　　　　By his own interdiction stands accursed
　　　　And does blaspheme his breed? Thy royal father
　　　　Was a most sainted king; the queen that bore thee,
　　　　Oft'ner upon her knees than on her feet,　　110
　　　　Died every day she lived. Fare thee well,
　　　　These evils thou repeat'st upon thyself
　　　　Hath banished me from Scotland. O my breast,
　　　　Thy hope ends here.
MALCOLM　　　　　　　Macduff, this noble passion,
　　　　Child of integrity, hath from my soul　　115
　　　　Wiped the black scruples, reconciled my thoughts
　　　　To thy good truth and honour. Devilish Macbeth
　　　　By many of these trains hath sought to win me
　　　　Into his power, and modest wisdom plucks me
　　　　From over-credulous haste; but God above　　120
　　　　Deal between thee and me, for even now
　　　　I put myself to thy direction and
　　　　Unspeak mine own detraction, here abjure
　　　　The taints and blames I laid upon myself,
　　　　For strangers to my nature. I am yet　　125
　　　　Unknown to woman, never was forsworn,

Malcolm asserts his virtue and declares he is now ready to invade Scotland. The Doctor tells how King Edward cures sick people by his touch. Malcolm says the gift of healing is passed down to future kings.

1 'Why are you silent?'

What is Macduff thinking at this moment (line 137) after Malcolm has just revealed he's only been testing him? Some productions make Macduff's disorientation a comic moment, but might Macduff's reply suggest that he now feels unsure about the alliance with Malcolm?

2 Curing the sick (in groups of six or more)

'The Evil' (or King's Evil) was scrofula, a type of tuberculosis. It was thought that the 'strangely visited' (very sick people) could be cured by the touch of the king, who would then hang a 'stamp' (coin or medal) round their neck.

Prepare a presentation of the ceremony described in lines 149–56. End your ceremony with a prophecy spoken by the king (line 159) about Malcolm and Macbeth.

3 Dramatic contrast

Some critics argue that the Doctor's lines were inserted to flatter King James I (who did not actually believe in the practice of 'touching'). But there are dramatic reasons for this episode. It establishes a contrast of the two kings: Macbeth is dedicated to destruction, King Edward to healing. The images of saintliness ('holy prayers', 'healing benediction', 'sundry blessings', 'full of grace') reinforce the contrasting impression that Edward, unlike Macbeth, is a king concerned for his nation's moral and spiritual health.

coveted   desired
here-approach   arrival here
at a point   prepared for war
stay his cure   await his healing touch
their malady . . . art   illnesses defeat
  the efforts of medical science

sanctity   holiness
here-remain   stay
solicits   entreats
benediction   blessing
With . . . virtue   in addition to this
  unusual quality

Scarcely have coveted what was mine own,
At no time broke my faith, would not betray
The devil to his fellow, and delight
No less in truth than life. My first false speaking   130
Was this upon myself. What I am truly
Is thine, and my poor country's, to command:
Whither indeed, before thy here-approach,
Old Siward with ten thousand warlike men
Already at a point was setting forth.   135
Now we'll together, and the chance of goodness
Be like our warranted quarrel. Why are you silent?

MACDUFF Such welcome and unwelcome things at once,
'Tis hard to reconcile.

Enter a DOCTOR

MALCOLM   Well, more anon. –
Comes the king forth, I pray you?   140

DOCTOR Ay, sir: there are a crew of wretched souls
That stay his cure; their malady convinces
The great assay of art, but at his touch,
Such sanctity hath heaven given his hand,
They presently amend.   *Exit*   145

MALCOLM I thank you, doctor.

MACDUFF What's the disease he means?

MALCOLM 'Tis called the Evil.
A most miraculous work in this good king,
Which often since my here-remain in England   150
I have seen him do. How he solicits heaven
Himself best knows, but strangely visited people
All swoll'n and ulcerous, pitiful to the eye,
The mere despair of surgery, he cures,
Hanging a golden stamp about their necks   155
Put on with holy prayers, and 'tis spoken
To the succeeding royalty he leaves
The healing benediction. With this strange virtue,
He hath a heavenly gift of prophecy,
And sundry blessings hang about his throne   160
That speak him full of grace.

Enter ROSS

MACDUFF   See who comes here.

Ross reports that in Scotland suffering goes unremarked and good men's lives are short. He says that Macduff's family is well. Rebellion against Macbeth is rumoured. Malcolm reveals his plan to invade Scotland.

1 'Alas, poor country' (in pairs)

In lines 166–75 Ross tells what Scotland is like under Macbeth's rule. It is a country 'Almost afraid to know itself', uncertain of its own identity. Life has become so full of suffering that 'violent sorrow' has become commonplace. Death is so much a fact of everyday experience that good men are more vulnerable than plucked flowers: they do not live as long.

Take turns to speak Ross's lines, experimenting with different styles of delivery. (For example, does he speak in sadness or in anger?)

2 Bringing bad news (in pairs)

Ross knows what has happened to Macduff's family. But he does not immediately tell his terrible news, saying rather that they are 'well' and 'at peace'. Why does he delay? Step into role as Ross and Macduff and speak their dialogue in lines 178–82. Afterwards, talk together about why Ross avoids telling the dreadful news here.

3 Pacing the scene – emphasising key words

Every theatre director attempts to ensure that actors vary the pace at which words are spoken, and that they emphasise each word appropriately. Work through the page opposite and write notes on the pace and tone of each speech. Identify words you think should be given special emphasis. Remember that pauses can have as much significance as the spoken word itself. Suggest where pauses could be made to intensify dramatic effect.

---

betimes swiftly
not marked go unnoticed
A modern ecstasy everyday feeling
knell death bell
relation / Too nice too accurate a story
doth hiss the speaker is just stale news

teems gives birth to
niggard miser
out in rebellion
afoot marching
eye presence
doff remove

MALCOLM My countryman, but yet I know him not.

MACDUFF My ever gentle cousin, welcome hither.

MALCOLM I know him now. Good God betimes remove
　　　　The means that makes us strangers.

ROSS　　　　　　　　　　　　　　　Sir, amen.　　　165

MACDUFF Stands Scotland where it did?

ROSS　　　　　　　　　　　　　Alas, poor country,
　　　　Almost afraid to know itself. It cannot
　　　　Be called our mother, but our grave, where nothing,
　　　　But who knows nothing, is once seen to smile;
　　　　Where sighs, and groans, and shrieks that rend the air　170
　　　　Are made, not marked; where violent sorrow seems
　　　　A modern ecstasy. The deadman's knell
　　　　Is there scarce asked for who, and good men's lives
　　　　Expire before the flowers in their caps,
　　　　Dying or ere they sicken.

MACDUFF　　　　　　　　　　O relation　　　175
　　　　Too nice, and yet too true.

MALCOLM　　　　　　　　　What's the newest grief?

ROSS That of an hour's age doth hiss the speaker;
　　　　Each minute teems a new one.

MACDUFF　　　　　　　　　　How does my wife?

ROSS Why, well.

MACDUFF　　　And all my children?

ROSS　　　　　　　　　　　Well, too.

MACDUFF The tyrant has not battered at their peace?　　　180

ROSS No, they were well at peace when I did leave 'em.

MACDUFF Be not a niggard of your speech: how goes't?

ROSS When I came hither to transport the tidings
　　　　Which I have heavily borne, there ran a rumour
　　　　Of many worthy fellows that were out,　　　185
　　　　Which was to my belief witnessed the rather
　　　　For that I saw the tyrant's power afoot.
　　　　Now is the time of help. [*To Malcolm*] Your eye in
　　　　　　Scotland
　　　　Would create soldiers, make our women fight
　　　　To doff their dire distresses.

MALCOLM　　　　　　　　　Be't their comfort　　　190
　　　　We are coming thither. Gracious England hath
　　　　Lent us good Siward and ten thousand men –

Ross tells of the murder of Macduff's family. Malcolm tries to comfort Macduff, who struggles with his grief over the slaughter of his wife and children.

1 Telling the terrible news (in groups of three)

Take parts as Ross, Macduff and Malcolm and speak everything from line 195 ('But I have words') to the end of the scene. Notice that Ross still delays, then reports bluntly in lines 206–7. Also notice how Macduff presses for detail, then incredulously repeats 'all' four times in lines 218–21 as if he is unable to believe the enormity of what has happened.

Ross (left) tells Macduff of the death of his family. At what line opposite do you think this photograph was taken?

latch catch	**o'erfraught** overburdened
The general cause everyone	**hell-kite** bird of prey from Hell
fee-grief personal sorrow	**dam** mother
heaviest saddest	**fell swoop** deadly attack
quarry heap of slaughtered animals	

An older and a better soldier none
That Christendom gives out.
ROSS   Would I could answer
This comfort with the like. But I have words   195
That would be howled out in the desert air,
Where hearing should not latch them.
MACDUFF   What concern they?
The general cause, or is it a fee-grief
Due to some single breast?
ROSS   No mind that's honest
But in it shares some woe, though the main part   200
Pertains to you alone.
MACDUFF   If it be mine,
Keep it not from me; quickly let me have it.
ROSS Let not your ears despise my tongue forever
Which shall possess them with the heaviest sound
That ever yet they heard.
MACDUFF   H'm – I guess at it.   205
ROSS Your castle is surprised; your wife and babes
Savagely slaughtered. To relate the manner
Were on the quarry of these murdered deer
To add the death of you.
MALCOLM   Merciful heaven –
What, man, ne'er pull your hat upon your brows: 210
Give sorrow words; the grief that does not speak,
Whispers the o'erfraught heart and bids it break.
MACDUFF My children too?
ROSS   Wife, children, servants, all
That could be found.
MACDUFF   And I must be from thence?
My wife killed too?
ROSS   I have said.
MALCOLM   Be comforted.   215
Let's make us med'cines of our great revenge
To cure this deadly grief.
MACDUFF He has no children. All my pretty ones?
Did you say all? O hell-kite! All?
What, all my pretty chickens and their dam   220
At one fell swoop?

Macduff cannot hide his grief. He feels that he is to blame for his family's death. He vows vengeance on Macbeth. Malcolm declares that the time is ripe to overthrow Macbeth, as Heaven itself is against him.

1 What is a man? (in pairs)

Planning the murder of Duncan, Lady Macbeth had taunted Macbeth for not behaving like 'a man', and at the banquet she had accused him of being 'unmanned'. Now Malcolm (lines 222 and 238) and Macduff (line 224) express different interpretations of what it is to be a man. Talk together about what Malcolm and Macduff have in mind as they speak.

2 Malcolm's motivation

Earlier in the scene, Malcolm had engaged in a deception to test Macduff's integrity. His words now pose a moral question. Is Malcolm genuinely trying to help Macduff cope with his grief, or is he seizing an opportunity to urge him into the common cause against Macbeth? Step into role as Malcolm and write a letter to Donaldbain in Ireland telling him why you behaved as you did throughout this scene.

3 The longest scene (in small groups)

Either some productions of *Macbeth* do not present this scene on stage. Imagine you are about to put on the play. Split your group in half. One side argues for cutting the scene, the other for keeping it. Listen carefully to your opponents' reasons to cut or not to cut, and try to answer them.

Or this is the longest scene in the play. Explore ways of presenting it in the briefest time, but including all its major elements.

Naught wicked
demerits faults
whetstone sharpening stone
braggart boaster
intermission interval of time
Front to front face to face

Our lack . . . leave we have only to make our farewells
powers above angels
instruments trumpets (or weapons, or soldiers)

MALCOLM Dispute it like a man.

MACDUFF I shall do so;
But I must also feel it as a man;
I cannot but remember such things were   225
That were most precious to me. Did heaven look on,
And would not take their part? Sinful Macduff,
They were all struck for thee. Naught that I am,
Not for their own demerits but for mine,
Fell slaughter on their souls. Heaven rest them now.   230

MALCOLM Be this the whetstone of your sword, let grief
Convert to anger. Blunt not the heart, enrage it.

MACDUFF O, I could play the woman with mine eyes
And braggart with my tongue. But gentle heavens,
Cut short all intermission. Front to front   235
Bring thou this fiend of Scotland and myself;
Within my sword's length set him. If he scape,
Heaven forgive him too.

MALCOLM   This tune goes manly.
Come, go we to the king; our power is ready;
Our lack is nothing but our leave. Macbeth   240
Is ripe for shaking, and the powers above
Put on their instruments. Receive what cheer you may:
The night is long that never finds the day.

Exeunt

Looking back at Act 4
Activities for groups or individuals

1 Dramatic range: Macbeth's character?

The three scenes of Act 4 contain great dramatic range:

Ritual the Witches around the cauldron
Spectacle the Apparitions and the show of eight kings
Domestic family life Lady Macduff and her son
Horrific violation the murders in Macduff's castle
Deception and moral complexity Malcolm's testing of Macduff
Deep personal grief Macduff hears of his family's slaughter

Macbeth appears only in the second half of Scene 1, but each of the above episodes relates to him in some way. Write a paragraph on each showing how it expresses something significant about Macbeth himself.

2 A tempting letter from Macbeth

In Scene 3 Malcolm says that Macbeth has tried to lure him with offers of women, money and other incentives (lines 117–20). Write a letter from Macbeth tempting Malcolm to return to Scotland.

3 'How many children had Lady Macbeth?'

'He has no children', cries Macduff in Scene 3 as he is advised to seek revenge on Macbeth. But in Act 1 Scene 7 Lady Macbeth says that she has suckled a child at her breast. The critic L. C. Knights wrote a famous essay titled 'How many children had Lady Macbeth?'. His answer was that the question is unimportant, because *Macbeth* should be studied as a dramatic poem, rather than as a study of characters. But some productions of *Macbeth* have made 'children' a central concept. What is your view? Does it matter, in the play, whether she has children or not?

4 What is a traitor?

For Macbeth, Macduff is a traitor. But whether someone is 'a traitor' or 'a freedom fighter' depends on who is using the label. Who would you call 'a traitor' in the play? Why?

5 Different views of the Witches

Over the centuries, the Witches have been portrayed on stage in very different ways. Below are three versions. The first is a woodcut of 1619 showing three witches with their familiars. The second (top right) shows a traditional presentation of the witches around the cauldron. The third is from a production in 2000. Compare them with the illustrations on pages vi, 10, 102 and 178, then write (or design) how you would present them on stage.

6 Imagery

Act 4, like the whole play, is rich in imagery. Choose two or three images from each scene and write how each contributes to dramatic effect in creating atmosphere or character.

The Gentlewoman reports to the Doctor that she has seen Lady Macbeth sleepwalking. She refuses to tell what her mistress has said in her sleep. Lady Macbeth, asleep, enters with a candle.

1 Staging the scene (in groups of three)

This is one of the most famous scenes in world drama. Work out how you would stage it to maximum dramatic effect by preparing notes for the actors. Then act it!

2 What did Lady Macbeth write?

The Gentlewoman tells how she has seen Lady Macbeth carefully take paper, fold it, write on it, read it, and seal it – all in her sleep. What did Lady Macbeth write? A letter to Macbeth? A confession? Her will? A warning to Lady Macduff? Or . . . ? Write Lady Macbeth's document.

'Yet here's a spot.' Lady Macbeth in a Taiwanese adaptation, *The Kingdom of Desire*. It is ironic that after Duncan's murder, when Macbeth spoke obsessively of murdering sleep, Lady Macbeth dismissed his anxiety as 'brain-sickly'. She has now become sick in her own mind, and walks in her sleep.

the field the battlefield	**meet** fitting
closet chest for valuables	**taper** candle
perturbation disturbance	**guise** custom
watching waking	**seem** appear to be
slumbery agitation sleepwalking	**set down** write

Act 5 Scene 1
A room in Dunsinane Castle

Enter a DOCTOR OF PHYSIC, *and a* WAITING-GENTLEWOMAN

DOCTOR I have two nights watched with you, but can perceive no
truth in your report. When was it she last walked?

GENTLEWOMAN Since his majesty went into the field, I have seen
her rise from her bed, throw her night-gown upon her, unlock
her closet, take forth paper, fold it, write upon't, read it, after-   5
wards seal it, and again return to bed, yet all this while in a
most fast sleep.

DOCTOR A great perturbation in nature, to receive at once the
benefit of sleep and do the effects of watching. In this slumbery
agitation, besides her walking and other actual performances,   10
what at any time have you heard her say?

GENTLEWOMAN That, sir, which I will not report after her.

DOCTOR You may to me, and 'tis most meet you should.

GENTLEWOMAN Neither to you, nor anyone, having no witness to
confirm my speech.   15

Enter LADY [MACBETH], *with a taper*

Lo you, here she comes. This is her very guise and, upon my
life, fast asleep. Observe her, stand close.

DOCTOR How came she by that light?

GENTLEWOMAN Why, it stood by her. She has light by her con-
tinually, 'tis her command.   20

DOCTOR You see her eyes are open.

GENTLEWOMAN Ay, but their sense are shut.

DOCTOR What is it she does now? Look how she rubs her hands.

GENTLEWOMAN It is an accustomed action with her, to seem thus
washing her hands; I have known her continue in this a quarter   25
of an hour.

LADY MACBETH Yet here's a spot.

DOCTOR Hark, she speaks; I will set down what comes from her to
satisfy my remembrance the more strongly.

Lady Macbeth, fast asleep, tries to wash imagined blood from her hands. Her fragmented language echoes her own and Macbeth's words about past murders: Duncan, Lady Macduff, Banquo.

1 Dream – or nightmare? (in pairs)

Lady Macbeth's tortured imagination roams over past events: the bell ('One, two'); what she said to Macbeth before Duncan's murder; the sight of Duncan's bloodstained body; Lady Macduff's murder ('The Thane of Fife had a wife'); Banquo's ghost at the banquet; the knocking at the gate. Her obsession with washing illusory blood off her hands ironically contrasts with what she had said to Macbeth after Duncan's murder, 'A little water clears us of this deed'.

a One person speaks all Lady Macbeth says in lines 30–58. After each sentence the other person suggests what incident she is recalling or imagining.

b Take turns to speak her lines, accompanying the words with appropriate actions.

You mar all with this starting you spoil everything with your nervousness (see Act 3 Scene 4, line 63)
sorely charged heavily burdened
the dignity of the whole body the sake of life itself

Foul whisp'rings are abroad terrible rumours are circulating
divine priest
still always
mated confused

LADY MACBETH Out, damned spot! Out, I say! One, two. Why 30
then 'tis time to do't. Hell is murky. Fie, my lord, fie, a soldier,
and afeard? What need we fear? Who knows it, when none can
call our power to account? Yet who would have thought the old
man to have had so much blood in him?

DOCTOR Do you mark that? 35

LADY MACBETH The Thane of Fife had a wife. Where is she
now? What, will these hands ne'er be clean? No more o'that,
my lord, no more o'that. You mar all with this starting.

DOCTOR Go to, go to; you have known what you should not.

GENTLEWOMAN She has spoke what she should not, I am sure of 40
that. Heaven knows what she has known.

LADY MACBETH Here's the smell of the blood still; all the perfumes of Arabia will not sweeten this little hand. O, O, O.

DOCTOR What a sigh is there! The heart is sorely charged.

GENTLEWOMAN I would not have such a heart in my bosom for 45
the dignity of the whole body.

DOCTOR Well, well, well –

GENTLEWOMAN Pray God it be, sir.

DOCTOR This disease is beyond my practice; yet I have known
those which have walked in their sleep who have died holily in 50
their beds.

LADY MACBETH Wash your hands, put on your night-gown, look
not so pale. I tell you yet again, Banquo's buried; he cannot
come out on's grave.

DOCTOR Even so? 55

LADY MACBETH To bed, to bed; there's knocking at the gate.
Come, come, come, come, give me your hand; what's done
cannot be undone. To bed, to bed, to bed. *Exit*

DOCTOR Will she go now to bed?

GENTLEWOMAN Directly. 60

DOCTOR Foul whisp'rings are abroad; unnatural deeds
Do breed unnatural troubles; infected minds
To their deaf pillows will discharge their secrets.
More needs she the divine than the physician.
God, God forgive us all. Look after her; 65
Remove from her the means of all annoyance,
And still keep eyes upon her. So, good night,
My mind she has mated, and amazed my sight.
I think, but dare not speak.

GENTLEWOMAN   Good night, good doctor.

                                                    Exeunt

News! Malcolm, Macduff, Siward and the English army approach; young men flock to join them; Macbeth is troubled by internal revolt – his soldiers obey him only out of fear, and his conscience oppresses him.

---

1 Hope! (in groups of four)

The four thanes are full of hope because of Macbeth's difficulties and the approach of Malcolm's army. They can see, not far ahead, freedom from tyranny. Speak lines 1–31 in two ways:

- Take parts as the four thanes and read through the scene.
- Do not take parts, but take turns to read up to a punctuation mark, then hand on. Speak in whispers, as conspirators.

Which reading most powerfully conveys a sense of mounting optimism?

2 Views of Macbeth (in small groups)

One person reads lines 12–25, speaking a short section at a time. The others mime each description of Macbeth (some are easy to present as actions, others will take longer to work out).

3 Clothing

Lines 15–16 and 20–2 use images of clothing to describe Macbeth. Imagine you are a cartoonist on a Scottish newspaper. Produce a cartoon of Macbeth using one or other of these images. Add a suitable caption.

4 A soldier's view

Ordinary people don't get much of a voice in the play. Step into role as a Scottish soldier who overhears the four thanes' conversation. Write a letter home telling your own version of what is said in Scene 2.

---

colours flags, banners
Excite the mortified man bring the dead back to life
file list
unrough . . . manhood unbearded young men, inexperienced in battle
distempered cause diseased regime

Now minutely . . . faith-breach every minute there's a rebellion protesting against his treachery
the med'cine . . . weal Malcolm (the cure of the diseased kingdom)
purge cure by cleansing

Act 5 Scene 2
Scotland Open country

Drum and colours. Enter MENTEITH, CAITHNESS, ANGUS,
LENNOX, Soldiers

MENTEITH The English power is near, led on by Malcolm,
His uncle Siward, and the good Macduff.
Revenges burn in them, for their dear causes
Would to the bleeding and the grim alarm
Excite the mortified man.

ANGUS   Near Birnam Wood   5
Shall we well meet them; that way are they coming.

CAITHNESS Who knows if Donaldbain be with his brother?

LENNOX For certain, sir, he is not. I have a file
Of all the gentry; there is Siward's son
And many unrough youths that even now   10
Protest their first of manhood.

MENTEITH   What does the tyrant?

CAITHNESS Great Dunsinane he strongly fortifies.
Some say he's mad; others that lesser hate him
Do call it valiant fury, but for certain
He cannot buckle his distempered cause   15
Within the belt of rule.

ANGUS   Now does he feel
His secret murders sticking on his hands.
Now minutely revolts upbraid his faith-breach;
Those he commands, move only in command,
Nothing in love. Now does he feel his title   20
Hang loose about him, like a giant's robe
Upon a dwarfish thief.

MENTEITH   Who then shall blame
His pestered senses to recoil and start,
When all that is within him does condemn
Itself for being there?

CAITHNESS   Well, march we on   25
To give obedience where 'tis truly owed;
Meet we the med'cine of the sickly weal,
And with him pour we in our country's purge,
Each drop of us.

Macbeth, receiving news of desertions from his army, recalls the Apparitions' predictions. He rages at a soldier who tells of Malcolm's approach. He knows the coming battle will make or break him.

---

1 'No more reports'

Every military commander relies on intelligence (reports about the enemy). Write several reports that Macbeth has received from his agents. Each brings him depressing news.

2 Deserters (in small groups)

'Let them fly all', cries Macbeth as he hears that more of his followers have deserted him. Improvise a conversation between a group of soldiers in Macbeth's army as they argue about whether or not to desert.

3 'Thou cream-faced loon' (in pairs)

A servant brings more bad news, and Macbeth's response is a series of insults (lines 11–17). Hurl the insults at each other! What do they tell you about the appearance of the unfortunate servant?

4 Macbeth's mood swings (in pairs)

Faced with bad news, Macbeth tries to cheer himself by recalling the words of the Apparitions ('Birnam Wood' and 'no man that's born of woman'). His mood was described in the previous scene as 'mad' or 'valiant fury'. His mood swings are evident in this scene. To help you find Macbeth's varying moods, speak all he says in lines 1–61. Share his lines between you, speaking sentences alternately.

Identify the points where Macbeth's mood and tone of voice change in the scene. Then prepare notes for an actor advising him how he might speak throughout the scene.

---

dew the sovereign flower restore the rightful king
taint become infected, weaken
mortal consequences human destiny
epicures luxury-lovers
sway by rule, control
push attack
cheer . . . disseat me comfort me or dethrone me

LENNOX   Or so much as it needs
              To dew the sovereign flower and drown the weeds.   30
              Make we our march towards Birnam.

                                        Exeunt, marching

Act 5 Scene 3
Dunsinane Castle

              Enter MACBETH, DOCTOR, and Attendants

MACBETH Bring me no more reports, let them fly all;
              Till Birnam Wood remove to Dunsinane,
              I cannot taint with fear. What's the boy Malcolm?
              Was he not born of woman? The spirits that know
              All mortal consequences have pronounced me thus: 5
              'Fear not, Macbeth, no man that's born of woman
              Shall e'er have power upon thee.' Then fly false thanes
              And mingle with the English epicures;
              The mind I sway by and the heart I bear
              Shall never sag with doubt nor shake with fear.   10

              Enter SERVANT

              The devil damn thee black, thou cream-faced loon.
              Where got'st thou that goose-look?
SERVANT There is ten thousand –
MACBETH   Geese, villain?
SERVANT   Soldiers, sir.
MACBETH Go prick thy face and over-red thy fear,
              Thou lily-livered boy. What soldiers, patch?   15
              Death of thy soul, those linen cheeks of thine
              Are counsellors to fear. What soldiers, whey-face?
SERVANT The English force, so please you.
MACBETH Take thy face hence!

                                        [*Exit Servant*]
                          Seyton! – I am sick at heart,
              When I behold – Seyton, I say! – this push   20
              Will cheer me ever or disseat me now.

Macbeth reflects on a bleak future. He determines to fight to the death, and orders rumour-mongers to be killed. When the Doctor tells him he cannot cure mental disorders, Macbeth dismisses medicine.

---

1 Not 'honour', but 'mouth-honour' (in pairs)

Macbeth wearily broods on the unhappy future that awaits him. In line 25 he lists four things that old people hope for, and in lines 27–8 two that he's likely to receive. Actors try to speak such 'lists' using a different tone of voice for each 'item'. Advise the actor how he could speak each word or phrase to bring out Macbeth's feeling about each.

2 Seyton = Satan? (in pairs)

In some productions of the play, Seyton is pronounced 'Satan' (King of Hell). Talk together about what you think that adds to the drama. Suggest how you would present Seyton: his costume and behaviour.

3 Shakespeare as Sigmund Freud? (in pairs)

Three hundred years before Sigmund Freud, Shakespeare seems to have invented psychoanalysis. Macbeth's description of 'a mind diseased' (lines 41–6) exactly catches the anxiety, depression and sorrow that Freud sought to cure by psychoanalysis. Freud's method, in essence, resembles what the Doctor says in lines 46–7: 'Therein the patient / Must minister to himself'. This expresses the heart of psychoanalytic practice: the patient, by talking through his or her problem with an analyst, effectively finds his or her own cure.

Psychoanalyse Lady Macbeth: one person as patient, one as psychoanalyst. The analyst asks questions to help Lady Macbeth find out what's troubling her.

---

sere withered
mouth-honour, breath lip service, flattery
fain gladly
skirr scour
thick-coming fancies frequent nightmares

minister to cure
Raze out the written troubles erase the deep anxieties
physic medicine
cast / The water analyse the urine
purge cure by cleansing
pristine fresh, original

I have lived long enough. My way of life
Is fall'n into the sere, the yellow leaf,
And that which should accompany old age,
As honour, love, obedience, troops of friends,　　　　　25
I must not look to have; but in their stead,
Curses, not loud but deep, mouth-honour, breath
Which the poor heart would fain deny, and dare not.
Seyton!

Enter SEYTON

SEYTON What's your gracious pleasure?
MACBETH　　　　　　　　　　　What news more?　　　　30
SEYTON All is confirmed, my lord, which was reported.
MACBETH I'll fight till from my bones my flesh be hacked.
　　　　Give me my armour.
SEYTON 'Tis not needed yet.
MACBETH I'll put it on;　　　　　　　　　　　　　　35
　　　　Send out more horses; skirr the country round.
　　　　Hang those that talk of fear. Give me mine armour.
　　　　How does your patient, doctor?
DOCTOR　　　　　　　　　　　Not so sick, my lord,
　　　　As she is troubled with thick-coming fancies
　　　　That keep her from her rest.
MACBETH　　　　　　　　　　　Cure her of that.　　　　40
　　　　Canst thou not minister to a mind diseased,
　　　　Pluck from the memory a rooted sorrow,
　　　　Raze out the written troubles of the brain,
　　　　And with some sweet oblivious antidote
　　　　Cleanse the stuffed bosom of that perilous stuff　　45
　　　　Which weighs upon the heart?
DOCTOR　　　　　　　　　　　Therein the patient
　　　　Must minister to himself.
MACBETH Throw physic to the dogs, I'll none of it.
　　　　Come, put mine armour on; give me my staff. –
　　　　Seyton, send out. – Doctor, the thanes fly from me. –　50
　　　　[*To Attendant*] Come sir, dispatch. – If thou couldst,
　　　　　　doctor, cast
　　　　The water of my land, find her disease,
　　　　And purge it to a sound and pristine health,
　　　　I would applaud thee to the very echo

Macbeth leaves, calling for his armour. The Doctor determines to desert. Malcolm orders the army to use branches to camouflage their approach to Dunsinane. He reports many desertions from Macbeth's army.

Gustave Doré's 1870 vision of Malcolm's army advancing, screened by branches from Birnam Wood. Work out how, in your own production, you could stage the approach of the camouflaged army.

cynne senna, a plant to purge (cleanse) the body
bane ruin
chambers bedrooms (Duncan was murdered in his bedroom)
shadow conceal
discovery / Err in report of us reconnaissance reports wrong about our numbers

setting down before't siege
advantage to be given opportunity to escape
more and less . . . revolt nobles and ordinary soldiers have deserted him
constrainèd things unwilling conscript soldiers

That should applaud again. – Pull't off, I say! –   55
What rhubarb, cynne, or what purgative drug
Would scour these English hence? Hear'st thou of them?
DOCTOR Ay, my good lord; your royal preparation
Makes us hear something.
MACBETH   Bring it after me. –
I will not be afraid of death and bane,   60
Till Birnam Forest come to Dunsinane.

                              [*Exeunt all but Doctor*]
DOCTOR Were I from Dunsinane away and clear,
Profit again should hardly draw me here.   *Exit*

Act 5 Scene 4
Near Birnam Wood

Drum and colours. Enter MALCOLM, SIWARD, MACDUFF,
Siward's son, MENTEITH, CAITHNESS, ANGUS, and SOLDIERS,
marching

MALCOLM Cousins, I hope the days are near at hand
That chambers will be safe.
MENTEITH   We doubt it nothing.
SIWARD What wood is this before us?
MENTEITH   The Wood of Birnam.
MALCOLM Let every soldier hew him down a bough,
And bear't before him; thereby shall we shadow   5
The numbers of our host and make discovery
Err in report of us.
A SOLDIER   It shall be done.
SIWARD We learn no other, but the confident tyrant
Keeps still in Dunsinane and will endure
Our setting down before't.
MALCOLM   'Tis his main hope,   10
For where there is advantage to be given,
Both more and less have given him the revolt,
And none serve with him but constrainèd things
Whose hearts are absent too.

Siward advises against over-optimism. Macbeth defies the siege. Only desertions stop him openly facing Malcolm's army. He has almost lost any sense of fear. Seyton brings news of Lady Macbeth's death.

---

1 Scene contrast, speech contrast

Scene 4 dramatically contrasts with Scene 3 in that Macbeth's reliance on the Apparition's forecast that he would not be defeated until Birnam Wood came to Dunsinane was followed by Malcolm's order to his soldiers to cut branches from Birnam Wood as camouflage. Now Shakespeare ends Scene 4 with Macduff's calm call for 'Industrious soldiership', then provides an immediate contrast by opening Scene 5 with Macbeth's bravado. As you read on, look out for other contrasts that add to dramatic effect.

2 'I have supped full with horrors' (in pairs)

The sound of women mourning prompts Macbeth to reflect that he has lost almost all sense of fear. Once, an owl's shriek or a horror story would make his blood run cold and his hair stand on end. Now he can no longer be frightened. Take turns to speak lines 9–15, to bring out the difference in tone from his first speech in this scene.

3 'The queen, my lord, is dead' (in pairs)

How did Lady Macbeth die? At the end of the play, Malcolm reports that she committed suicide, but that may not be true (because history is written by the victors). Talk together about how you think she might have met her death, then

Either write her dying speech

Or write an interview with her Gentlewoman (from Scene 1), imagining her story.

---

just censures ... event   rightful claims decide the result
owe   own, have won
Thoughts speculative ... arbitrate   thinking won't determine the matter, but battle will
ague   fever

forced   reinforced
my fell of hair   every hair on my body
treatise   story
Direness   horror
slaughterous   murderous
start   frighten

MACDUFF   Let our just censures
      Attend the true event and put we on   15
      Industrious soldiership.
SIWARD   The time approaches
      That will with due decision make us know
      What we shall say we have and what we owe;
      Thoughts speculative their unsure hopes relate,
      But certain issue strokes must arbitrate.   20
      Towards which, advance the war.

Exeunt, marching

Act 5 Scene 5
Dunsinane Castle

Enter MACBETH, SEYTON, *and Soldiers, with drum and colours*

MACBETH Hang out our banners on the outward walls;
      The cry is still, 'They come.' Our castle's strength
      Will laugh a siege to scorn; here let them lie
      Till famine and the ague eat them up.
      Were they not forced with those that should be ours,   5
      We might have met them dareful, beard to beard,
      And beat them backward home.
      A cry within of women
                          What is that noise?
SEYTON It is the cry of women, my good lord.
MACBETH I have almost forgot the taste of fears;
      The time has been, my senses would have cooled   10
      To hear a night-shriek and my fell of hair
      Would at a dismal treatise rouse and stir
      As life were in't. I have supped full with horrors;
      Direness familiar to my slaughterous thoughts
      Cannot once start me. Wherefore was that cry?   15
SEYTON The queen, my lord, is dead.

His wife's death sets Macbeth brooding on life's futility. A messenger tells that Birnam Wood is moving towards Dunsinane. Macbeth doubts the Apparition's ambiguous words. He determines to die fighting.

---

1 'Tomorrow, and tomorrow, and tomorrow' (in pairs)

In lines 18–27 Macbeth wearily speaks of time past, present and future and of how fragile and empty he finds human life. It is less than a flickering light ('brief candle') or an actor's 'hour', posturing on stage. Like an absurd and pointless tale told by an idiot, it signifies 'nothing'. It is worthwhile spending a good deal of time exploring this world-famous speech. Work on one or more of the following:

a Speak it in different ways (for example, sadly, wonderingly).

b Whisper the lines to each other as though telling a secret message.

c Express them as world-weary, bleak fatalism.

d Decide to whom he speaks. (To himself? Seyton? The audience? Or . . . ?)

e Devise actions and expressions for each section.

f Talk together about the imagery Macbeth uses. What makes it so memorable?

g Write notes advising the actor how to deliver the lines on stage.

2 'The wood began to move' (in pairs)

After Macbeth's bleak reflections on human life, the pace of the action quickens. Macbeth reacts to the news of Birnam Wood moving with a mixture of threat, doubt, weariness and bravado. Take turns to speak lines 28–51 as the Messenger and Macbeth. Use your experience of speaking the lines to identify the points where Macbeth's mood changes.

---

watch period of guard duty
anon soon
cling wither
sooth true
I pull in resolution I lose my firmness of purpose

equivocation double-talk
avouches says is true
tarrying waiting
th'estate o'th'world the universe
wrack destruction
harness armour

MACBETH   She should have died hereafter;
          There would have been a time for such a word.
          Tomorrow, and tomorrow, and tomorrow
          Creeps in this petty pace from day to day
          To the last syllable of recorded time;   20
          And all our yesterdays have lighted fools
          The way to dusty death. Out, out, brief candle,
          Life's but a walking shadow, a poor player
          That struts and frets his hour upon the stage
          And then is heard no more. It is a tale   25
          Told by an idiot, full of sound and fury
          Signifying nothing.

                    Enter a MESSENGER

          Thou com'st to use thy tongue: thy story quickly.
MESSENGER Gracious my lord,
          I should report that which I say I saw,   30
          But know not how to do't.
MACBETH   Well, say, sir.
MESSENGER As I did stand my watch upon the hill
          I looked toward Birnam and anon methought
          The wood began to move.
MACBETH   Liar and slave!
MESSENGER Let me endure your wrath if't be not so;   35
          Within this three mile may you see it coming.
          I say, a moving grove.
MACBETH   If thou speak'st false,
          Upon the next tree shall thou hang alive
          Till famine cling thee; if thy speech be sooth,
          I care not if thou dost for me as much.   40
          I pull in resolution and begin
          To doubt th'equivocation of the fiend
          That lies like truth. 'Fear not, till Birnam Wood
          Do come to Dunsinane', and now a wood
          Comes toward Dunsinane. Arm, arm, and out!   45
          If this which he avouches does appear,
          There is nor flying hence nor tarrying here.
          I 'gin to be aweary of the sun
          And wish th'estate o'th'world were now undone.
          Ring the alarum bell! Blow wind, come wrack;   50
          At least we'll die with harness on our back.

                                             Exeunt

                                             147

Malcolm instructs his troops to throw aside their camouflage of branches. He issues orders for battle. Macbeth compares himself to a baited bear. He is challenged by Young Siward.

1 Battle plans

Malcolm orders the onslaught on Macbeth 'According to our order' (the battle plan, Scene 6 lines 1–6). Draw up the battle plan: it is usually a written order with a sketch-map.

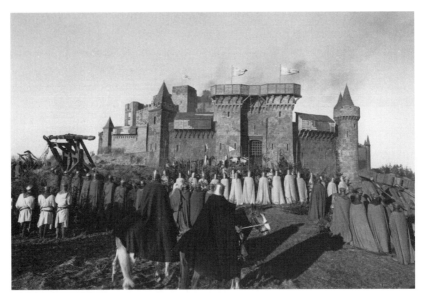

Films offer different opportunities from stage productions. Actual locations can be used, and battle scenes presented realistically with a cast of hundreds. The illustration is from Roman Polanski's 1971 film of the play, and shows the English army about to attack Macbeth's castle at Dunsinane. You will find an activity on page 154 inviting you to treat the battle scenes as a film script.

---

leafy screens   tree branches (camouflage)
clamorous harbingers   noisy forerunners (trumpet blasts)

Alarums   noise of battle
bear-like   chained like a baited bear
course   battle, period of trial

Act 5 Scene 6
Outside Dunsinane Castle

Drum and colours. Enter MALCOLM, SIWARD, MACDUFF, *and their army, with boughs*

MALCOLM Now near enough; your leafy screens throw down
    And show like those you are. You, worthy uncle,
    Shall with my cousin your right noble son
    Lead our first battle. Worthy Macduff and we
    Shall take upon's what else remains to do,   5
    According to our order.
SIWARD   Fare you well.
    Do we but find the tyrant's power tonight,
    Let us be beaten if we cannot fight.
MACDUFF Make all our trumpets speak; give them all breath,
    Those clamorous harbingers of blood and death.   10

                Exeunt
      Alarums continued

Act 5 Scene 7
Near the castle gate

Enter MACBETH

MACBETH They have tied me to a stake; I cannot fly,
    But bear-like I must fight the course. What's he
    That was not born of woman? Such a one
    Am I to fear, or none.

      Enter YOUNG SIWARD

YOUNG SIWARD What is thy name?   5
MACBETH Thou'lt be afraid to hear it.
YOUNG SIWARD No, though thou call'st thyself a hotter name
    Than any is in hell.

Macbeth kills Young Siward and boasts that no man born of woman can kill him. Macduff refuses to fight with mercenaries and seeks only Macbeth. Siward invites Malcolm to enter Macbeth's surrendered castle.

1 Stage-fighting (in small groups)

Many professional productions call on the services of a fight arranger who works out how a stage fight can be both dramatic and safe. Work out the moves for lines 5–14 in which Young Siward challenges Macbeth, but is slain by him. Remember that safety is vital, and rehearse the fight in slow motion.

2 Action and words (in small groups)

Macduff speaks lines 15–24 on an apparently empty stage, but most directors seek to create the impression that a battle is raging. They have to ensure that the lines can be heard and can be related to the action.

Take the lines a short section at a time, and decide what actions (or sounds) would fit best. You may wish other actors to come on stage at certain points, to give Macduff's sentences extra, visible meaning (for example where he refuses to fight with mercenaries: 'wretched kerns . . . staves').

3 'The tyrant's people on both sides do fight'

Some of Macbeth's soldiers have deserted and now fight for Malcolm (line 26). Step into role as one of the deserters and write your account of your experience in Macbeth's army, when and why you deserted, how you were received in Malcolm's army, and the part you played in the battle for the castle.

---

abhorrèd detested
kerns lightly armed soldiers
whose arms . . . staves mercenaries (who fight only for pay)
staves wooden weapons
undeeded unused (having performed no deeds)

one of greatest note (Macbeth)
bruited shouted about
gently rendered surrendered with little fighting
strike beside us deliberately miss us

MACBETH   My name's Macbeth.

YOUNG SIWARD The devil himself could not pronounce a title
     More hateful to mine ear.

MACBETH   No, nor more fearful.   10

YOUNG SIWARD Thou liest, abhorrèd tyrant; with my sword
     I'll prove the lie thou speak'st.

          Fight, and young Siward slain

MACBETH   Thou wast born of woman.
     But swords I smile at, weapons laugh to scorn,
     Brandished by man that's of a woman born.

               Exit [with young Siward's body]

         Alarums. Enter MACDUFF

MACDUFF That way the noise is. Tyrant, show thy face!   15
     If thou be'st slain, and with no stroke of mine,
     My wife and children's ghosts will haunt me still.
     I cannot strike at wretched kerns whose arms
     Are hired to bear their staves; either thou, Macbeth,
     Or else my sword with an unbattered edge   20
     I sheath again undeeded. There thou shouldst be;
     By this great clatter, one of greatest note
     Seems bruited. Let me find him, Fortune,
     And more I beg not.   *Exit*

        Alarums. Enter MALCOLM *and* SIWARD

SIWARD This way, my lord; the castle's gently rendered.   25
     The tyrant's people on both sides do fight;
     The noble thanes do bravely in the war.
     The day almost itself professes yours,
     And little is to do.

MALCOLM   We have met with foes
     That strike beside us.

SIWARD   Enter, sir, the castle.   30

                  Exeunt

      Alarum

Facing Macduff, Macbeth boasts that no naturally born man can kill him, but Macduff reveals his own Caesarean birth. Dismayed, Macbeth refuses to fight. Macduff threatens he will be exhibited in captivity.

'My voice is in my sword'. Macduff (left) finally encounters Macbeth.

1 'Juggling fiends'

Macbeth has been relying on the prophecy that he cannot be killed by 'one of woman born'. But Macduff's revelation that he was not born normally, but by Caesarean section, shatters Macbeth. He realises that he has been duped and mocked by the Witches and their Apparitions. The Witches have proved skilful equivocators (see p. 163); their lies have misled him. Suggest how Macbeth physically reacts to Macduff's 'Untimely ripped', and how he delivers lines 17–22.

play the Roman fool commit suicide (defeated Roman generals fell on their swords)
terms words
intrenchant uncuttable
impress mark, strike

crests helmets, heads
angel devil, Satan
Untimely ripped prematurely delivered (by Caesarean section)
palter with us in a double sense equivocate with double meanings

Act 5 Scene 8
Outside Dunsinane Castle

Enter MACBETH

MACBETH Why should I play the Roman fool and die
  On mine own sword? Whiles I see lives, the gashes
  Do better upon them.

Enter MACDUFF

MACDUFF   Turn, hell-hound, turn.
MACBETH Of all men else I have avoided thee,
  But get thee back, my soul is too much charged   5
  With blood of thine already.
MACDUFF   I have no words;
  My voice is in my sword, thou bloodier villain
  Than terms can give thee out.
       Fight. Alarum
MACBETH   Thou losest labour.
  As easy mayst thou the intrenchant air
  With thy keen sword impress as make me bleed.   10
  Let fall thy blade on vulnerable crests;
  I bear a charmèd life which must not yield
  To one of woman born.
MACDUFF   Despair thy charm,
  And let the angel whom thou still hast served
  Tell thee, Macduff was from his mother's womb   15
  Untimely ripped.
MACBETH Accursèd be that tongue that tells me so,
  For it hath cowed my better part of man;
  And be these juggling fiends no more believed
  That palter with us in a double sense,   20
  That keep the word of promise to our ear
  And break it to our hope. I'll not fight with thee.
MACDUFF Then yield thee coward,
  And live to be the show and gaze o'th'time.
  We'll have thee, as our rarer monsters are,   25
  Painted upon a pole and underwrit,
  'Here may you see the tyrant.'

Macbeth determines to go down fighting, and is killed. Siward reports light casualties. On being told that his son is dead, Siward's concern is to know if Young Siward died bravely.

1 Death rather than captivity (in pairs)

Macbeth realises that the end has come. The Apparitions have falsely raised his hopes by their double-talk. They have both lied and spoken the truth about Birnam Wood and 'no man of woman born'. Macbeth ends defiantly. He chooses to die fighting because he cannot bear the thought of being subservient to Malcolm and exhibited like a freak in a fairground show.

Speak lines 27–34 several times, then talk together about how Macbeth's choice affects your view of him. Does choosing death give him a kind of nobility and dignity, or is it just the animal instinct of someone who has despaired of life?

2 Shakespeare's film script? (in small groups)

Scenes 4–8 are like a film script: a series of brief, action-filled episodes. They show different aspects of the fighting, and build up a vivid impression of the fast-moving battle. Identify the different sequences in the five scenes, and write a film script. Alternatively, you could design a 'story board': a series of sketches illustrating each camera shot. Locate places in your school or college (or elsewhere) where you could shoot each episode.

3 Siward: soldier and father (in groups of three)

In Scene 9, Siward has to face the loss of his son in the battle. His response expresses his soldier's code of honour: what matters is that Young Siward died bravely. Take parts and read lines 1–20, then talk together about what you think this episode adds to the play, and your response to Siward's attitude to his son's death.

---

baited mocked, tormented like a chained bear
Retreat, and flourish trumpet call at the end of battle, fanfare
go off die
prowess bravery

unshrinking station place of no retreat
Had he his hurts before? Were his wounds on the front of his body? (Was he facing the enemy?)

MACBETH   I will not yield
    To kiss the ground before young Malcolm's feet
    And to be baited with the rabble's curse.
    Though Birnam Wood be come to Dunsinane   30
    And thou opposed being of no woman born,
    Yet I will try the last. Before my body,
    I throw my warlike shield. Lay on, Macduff,
    And damned be him that first cries, 'Hold, enough!'
                        Exeunt[,] *fighting. Alarums*

Enter [Macbeth and Macduff,] fighting[,] and Macbeth slain

               [Exit Macduff, with Macbeth's body]

Act 5   Scene 9
Dunsinane Castle

Retreat, and flourish. Enter with drum and colours, MALCOLM,
      SIWARD, ROSS, *Thanes, and Soldiers*

MALCOLM I would the friends we miss were safe arrived.
SIWARD Some must go off. And yet by these I see,
    So great a day as this is cheaply bought.
MALCOLM Macduff is missing and your noble son.
ROSS Your son, my lord, has paid a soldier's debt;   5
    He only lived but till he was a man,
    The which no sooner had his prowess confirmed
    In the unshrinking station where he fought,
    But like a man he died.
SIWARD   Then he is dead?
ROSS Ay, and brought off the field. Your cause of sorrow   10
    Must not be measured by his worth, for then
    It hath no end.
SIWARD   Had he his hurts before?
ROSS Ay, on the front.

Macduff displays Macbeth's severed head, and hails Malcolm as King of Scotland. Malcolm rewards his nobles for their services, creating them earls. He invites everyone to his coronation at Scone.

---

1 Macbeth's head

Often, audiences are not sure whether to be appalled or to laugh at the sight of Macbeth's severed head. Imagine you are the designer of a production. Decide what you will do about Macbeth's head.

2 Peace at last? Or . . .? (in large groups)

Malcolm's first act as king is to reward his followers with earldoms. Shakespeare may have King James I in mind; he also granted earldoms to his supporters when he became King of England. Malcolm's action may seem sensible, but earlier in the play Duncan's appointment of Macbeth as Thane of Cawdor prompted Macbeth's ambition, which led to murder and tyranny. Might the same thing happen with Malcolm's nobles?

That thought has led some critics to question whether Malcolm's victory restores peace, order, justice and harmony to Scotland. They argue that Scotland will still be torn apart by the power struggles of ambitious warlords. Prepare two versions of how Malcolm's final speech is received. One version shows the prospect of a peaceful future; the second shows a future of war and oppression.

3 Bring on the Witches (in large groups)

Some productions of the play have the Witches present at these final moments of the play. In one, they attended on Malcolm, marking him out as a future victim. In another, they picked at the corpse of Macbeth, the victim they had enticed to disaster. Work out your own presentation of lines 21–42 that includes the Witches.

---

knell is knolled   death bell is rung
paid his score   settled his account
(died as a man)
usurper   illegal king
**compassed with thy kingdom's
  pearl**   surrounded by the nobility
of Scotland

reckon with your several loves
  calculate what I owe each of you
be planted newly . . . time   begin the
  new era
watchful tyranny   Macbeth's
  totalitarian regime
ministers   supporters
by self . . . life   killed herself

SIWARD Why then, God's soldier be he;
　　　　Had I as many sons as I have hairs,　　　　　　　15
　　　　I would not wish them to a fairer death.
　　　　And so his knell is knolled.
MALCOLM　　　　　　　　　　He's worth more sorrow,
　　　　And that I'll spend for him.
SIWARD　　　　　　　　　　He's worth no more;
　　　　They say he parted well and paid his score,
　　　　And so God be with him. Here comes newer comfort.　　20

　　　　　　Enter MACDUFF, *with Macbeth's head*

MACDUFF Hail, king, for so thou art. Behold where stands
　　　　Th'usurper's cursèd head. The time is free.
　　　　I see thee compassed with thy kingdom's pearl,
　　　　That speak my salutation in their minds;
　　　　Whose voices I desire aloud with mine.　　　　　　25
　　　　Hail, King of Scotland.
ALL　　　　　　　　　　Hail, King of Scotland.
　　　　　　　　　　Flourish
MALCOLM We shall not spend a large expense of time
　　　　Before we reckon with your several loves
　　　　And make us even with you. My thanes and kinsmen,
　　　　Henceforth be earls, the first that ever Scotland　　30
　　　　In such an honour named. What's more to do
　　　　Which would be planted newly with the time, –
　　　　As calling home our exiled friends abroad
　　　　That fled the snares of watchful tyranny,
　　　　Producing forth the cruel ministers　　　　　　35
　　　　Of this dead butcher and his fiend-like queen,
　　　　Who, as 'tis thought, by self and violent hands
　　　　Took off her life, – this and what needful else
　　　　That calls upon us, by the grace of Grace
　　　　We will perform in measure, time, and place.　　40
　　　　So, thanks to all at once and to each one,
　　　　Whom we invite to see us crowned at Scone.
　　　　　　　　　　Flourish
　　　　　　　　　　　　　　　Exeunt
　　　　FINIS

Looking back at the play
Activities for groups or individuals

1 The Macbeths' changing relationship

In Acts 1 and 2 Lady Macbeth appeared confident and assertive, the dominant partner. But Act 3 suggests her growing separation from Macbeth, and lack of assurance. Act 5 shows their relationship severed as she retreats into exhausted nightmares. Select quotations to illustrate the changing relationship throughout the play.

2 A play of darkness

A pervasive sense of darkness intensifies the dramatic effect of the action and dialogue. Look back over the twenty-seven scenes and identify which you think take place at night or in darkness.

3 Three viewpoints: choose one

a Write the Scottish Doctor's case notes on Lady Macbeth.

b Write a letter from Lady Macbeth's Gentlewoman to her brother or sister, telling about her mistress.

c What happened to the 'cream-faced loon' of Act 5 Scene 3? Write his story of being Macbeth's servant in a castle under attack.

4 Appearance versus reality

Things are often not what they seem in *Macbeth*. The Witches seem to predict a prosperous future for Macbeth, but his mind becomes increasingly troubled, and his actions tyrannous. He and his wife put on false faces to deceive Duncan. Malcolm pretends to be villainous to test Macduff's sincerity. Even the branches of Birnam Wood are used to deceive, hiding Malcolm's army. Identify two or three examples in each act where appearance does not match reality. Use your examples as the basis for an essay on 'Appearance versus reality in *Macbeth*'.

5 Every picture tells a story

Look at the illustrations in this edition. Each has been chosen to help your understanding and inspire your imagination. Choose the five you like most, and write why each appeals to you.

6 A favourite scene

Choose one scene that you particularly enjoy. Step into role as director. Write detailed notes about how you would stage the scene to maximise dramatic effect.

Macbeth's luck (his 'charmèd life', Act 5 Scene 8, line 12) runs out as he is slain by Macduff. The play itself has gained a notorious reputation for being unlucky. Many actors refuse to speak its name, calling it instead 'the Scottish play', because they think the name *Macbeth* will bring bad luck. There are many stories of accidents associated with productions of the play. The worst was in May 1849 at a performance of *Macbeth* in New York. It provoked a bloody riot, which resulted in 22 deaths and over 150 injuries. Make a list of the features of the play (events, characters, and so on) which you think help create the view of it as 'unlucky'.

What is the play about?

Imagine that you can travel back in time to around 1606. You meet William Shakespeare a few minutes after he has finished writing *Macbeth*. You ask him 'What is the play about?'

Perhaps Shakespeare would reply, 'It's the story of a great Scottish soldier who is tempted into killing his king, taking the throne himself, and how he is overthrown. Or you can think of it as showing the mental and emotional turmoil of a man who is lured into evil and suffers the consequences.'

But the truth is that nobody can know how Shakespeare would reply. Like all great artists, Shakespeare doesn't seem interested in explaining his work. He leaves that up to others. Rather, he seems to say 'Here it is. Read it, perform it, make of it what you will.'

There has been no shortage of responses to that invitation! *Macbeth* has been hugely popular ever since it was first performed. The thousands of productions and millions of words written about it show that there is no single 'right way' of thinking about or performing the play. So it is impossible to reach a final answer to the question 'What is *Macbeth* about?'. The play is like a kaleidoscope. Every time it is performed it reveals different shapes, patterns, meanings, interpretations. For example, you could think about *Macbeth* as:

- a historical thriller – a fast-moving action-packed murder story
- a tragedy – the portrayal of the fall of a great man because of a fatal flaw in his character (Macbeth's ambition causes his death)
- a play of illusions – showing the effect on human beings of the mysterious and supernatural (the Witches, the dagger, and so on)
- a play of political and social realism – showing how an oppressive hierarchical society produces corrupt individuals
- a psychological study of a murderer's mind – Macbeth constantly reveals his troubled inmost thoughts
- a dramatic poem – showing how a poet-playwright of genius uses language to achieve remarkable imaginative and dramatic effects.

Another way of answering the question 'What is *Macbeth* about?' is to identify the themes of the play. Themes are ideas or concepts of fundamental importance that recur throughout the play, linking together plot, characters and language. Themes echo, reinforce, and comment upon each other and the whole play. The themes of *Macbeth* include:

Ambition Ruthless seeking after power by Macbeth, urged on by his equally ambitious wife. It can be thought of as the tragic flaw that causes his downfall ('I have no spur / To prick the sides of my intent, but only / Vaulting ambition').

Evil The brooding presence of murderous intention, destroying whatever is good. Macbeth's conscience troubles him, but he commits evil, and finds others to carry out his malign orders (murders of Duncan, Banquo, Lady Macduff).

Order and disorder The struggle to maintain or destroy social and natural bonds; the destruction of morality and mutual trust ('Uproar the universal peace, confound / All unity on earth').

Appearance versus reality Evil lurks behind fair looks. Deceit and hypocrisy mean that appearances cannot be trusted. The theme occurs throughout. It is introduced in the first scene as the Witches chant 'Fair is foul, and foul is fair'. Later in Act 1 Scene 5 Lady Macbeth urges Macbeth to 'look like th'innocent flower, / But be the serpent under't'.

Equivocation Telling half-truths with the intention to mislead ('th'equivocation of the fiend / That lies like truth').

Violence and tyranny Warfare, destruction and oppression recur throughout the play. In the first scene the Witches speak of 'the battle', and in the second the wounded Captain reports Macbeth's victory in a bloody war. Tempted by the prospect of becoming king, Macbeth embarks on a violent journey that makes him Scotland's tyrant. Malcolm expresses the theme in 'Pour the sweet milk of concord into hell'.

Guilt and conscience Macbeth knows what he does is wrong, but he does it none the less and suffers agonies of conscience as a result ('O, full of scorpions is my mind').

Man The violent feudal society of hierarchical male power breeds bloody stereotypes of what it is to be a man. 'I dare do all that may become a man', says Macbeth, contemplating murder. But the play offers other visions of manhood: 'But I must also feel it as a man', cries Macduff, weeping at news of his family's murder.

◆ Imagine you are asked to explain what *Macbeth* is about by an eight-year-old child, and also by your teacher/lecturer. Write a reply to each of them, using these two pages to help you.

The contexts of *Macbeth*

One way of thinking about *Macbeth* is to set it in the context of its time: the world that Shakespeare knew. His dramatic imagination was influenced by many features of that world. Three of those contexts are of particular importance: what he read, the dramatic tradition he knew about, and the monarch himself: King James I.

Shakespeare's reading   As he wrote *Macbeth*, Shakespeare had at his side a book published in 1587: *Chronicles of England, Scotland and Ireland* by Raphael Holinshed. Shakespeare had earlier used Holinshed's *Chronicles* extensively as the source for his English History plays. Now, he found in it the Scottish stories that his imagination would turn into the drama of *Macbeth*.

But Shakespeare never slavishly followed any source. Holinshed provided details of events, power politics, characters and motivations. Shakespeare selected, altered and added to achieve maximum dramatic effect. For example, he invented Lady Macbeth's sleepwalking and death, the banquet scene and Banquo's Ghost, and most of the cauldron scene. He changed Duncan from the ineffectual king that Holinshed presented into a respected and revered ruler. He makes Macbeth a tyrant immediately after he becomes king, ignoring Holinshed's account of Macbeth's ten years of good rule.

Shakespeare, unlike Holinshed, gives audiences full access to Macbeth's tortured mind, and vividly portrays the changing relationship of man and wife. He gives Lady Macbeth far greater prominence, inspired by Holinshed's brief comment: she 'was very ambitious, burning in unquenchable desire to bear the name of queen'.

Dramatic tradition   When Shakespeare first began to write plays, a strong influence was the popularity of the plays of the Roman playwright Seneca (4 BC–AD 65). Seneca's tragedies included soliloquies, ghosts, witches and magic, violent events, wrongs avenged, and moral statements. All those features can be found in *Macbeth*.

Some critics claim that *Macbeth* shows Shakespeare's recollection of Miracle plays: dramatised Bible stories which were immensely popular in the Middle Ages. One play is argued to be the inspiration of the Porter scene: *The Harrowing of Hell*. In it, Hell is a castle whose gate is guarded by a Porter named Rybald ('ribald' means coarse and vulgar). Christ descends to Hell and hammers on the gate, demanding that Satan release the good souls imprisoned there. In this interpretation of *Macbeth*, Macduff is the Christ-like figure who knocks at Macbeth's castle door. In Act 5 he enters the castle, kills the devil-tyrant, redeems Scotland and leads its people from darkness into light.

King James In 1603 James, King of Scotland and a member of the Stuart dynasty, succeeded Queen Elizabeth I on the English throne. Some critics argue that Shakespeare wrote *Macbeth* partly to flatter the new king (who probably saw a performance in 1606). It contains many echoes of James's interests:

Banquo Holinshed included an elaborate family tree of the Stuart dynasty, showing King James's descent from Banquo. Unlike Holinshed, Shakespeare did not make Banquo an accomplice to Duncan's murder. Instead, he makes the Macbeths solely responsible. This alteration presumably pleased King James, who hated regicides (king-killers). In fact, Banquo never existed. He was invented by historians as the source of Stuart royalty.

Witchcraft King James's interest in witchcraft was well known. He attended at least one witchcraft trial, read widely about the subject and published a book on it (see page 169). When he visited Oxford in 1605 he was greeted by three witches who hailed him as the descendant of Banquo.

The Gunpowder Plot, 5 November 1605 James's escape from being blown up was commemorated by a medal. It showed a snake concealed by flowers. The Plot may be referred to in Act 2 Scene 3, line 50 ('dire combustion'). Sir Everard Digby, one of the conspirators, was a favourite of James (mirroring the treacherous Thane of Cawdor?).

Equivocation In 1606 a Catholic priest, Henry Garnet, was accused of treason for involvement in the Gunpowder Plot. He was found to have committed perjury (lying on oath), but in self-defence claimed to have the right to equivocate (tell deliberately misleading half-truths). Equivocation is a major theme of the play, and Macbeth is frequently troubled by it, fearing that the Witches may have lied to him (see page 161).

Honours Malcolm's gift of earldoms at the end of the play reflects King James's liberal giving of English titles to his Scottish supporters. His action was resented by many of his new subjects, but the play gives no indication of that resentment.

◆ Which of the contexts given on these two pages most helps your understanding and appreciation of *Macbeth*? Why?

Characters

Macbeth appears first in the play as a military hero. King Duncan calls him 'valiant cousin, worthy gentleman', 'noble Macbeth', 'worthiest cousin'. He ends the play as a cruel tyrant, deserted by his soldiers and allies, and finally slain by Macduff. The new king, Malcolm, viewing Macbeth's severed head, dismisses him as 'this dead butcher'.

As he journeys through the play from brave soldier to murderous tyrant, Macbeth is revealed as a deeply sensitive man, tortured by his imagination and his conscience. His wife believes him to be a good man ('too full o'th'milk of human kindness') and he knows that it is wrong to kill Duncan. He struggles to overcome his evil thoughts, but is tempted to criminality by the Witches, by his wife's pressure, and by his own ambition. He murders his way to the throne of Scotland, and then arranges the killing of anyone he suspects to be his enemy.

Conflicting thoughts of good and evil constantly torment Macbeth ('O, full of scorpions is my mind, dear wife!'). But as he is drawn ever deeper into cruel and brutal actions he strives to harden his responses and to lose 'the taste of fears'. Learning of his wife's death, he reflects despairingly on the emptiness of life: 'a tale / Told by an idiot, full of sound and fury / Signifying nothing'.

He finally becomes aware that the Witches have misled him ('be these juggling fiends no more believed'). Even in his despair and weariness he determines to die bravely ('Blow wind, come wrack; / At least we'll die with harness on our back'). He slays Young Siward and, coming face to face with Macduff, still fights defiantly to the end although he realises he has met his nemesis ('Lay on, Macduff, / And damned be him that first cries, "Hold, enough"'). Whether Macbeth's final words and actions represent heroic endurance or the snarling of a trapped animal is open for each reader or new performance to decide.

◆ Study the picture opposite together with the other pictures of Macbeth in this edition, particularly those in the colour section. Then choose one or more of the 'character' activities on page 167.

Many well-known actors feel that they must play Macbeth at some stage in their career. In 2002 Sean Bean portrayed Macbeth as a tough soldier, deeply in love with his wife, torn by his loyalty to Duncan, but fatally tempted by the prospect of becoming king himself.

Lady Macbeth appears first as a supremely confident, dominant figure. She revels in the prospect of Macbeth becoming king, and calls on evil spirits to help her persuade him to kill Duncan. She urges him to use deception to cloak murderous intentions ('look like th'innocent flower, / But be the serpent under't'). When Macbeth's resolve to do the murder slackens, she taunts his manhood, convincing him to do the deed. She becomes his active accomplice, even returning the bloody daggers to Duncan's bedroom when Macbeth fears to return them himself.

In Act 3 Lady Macbeth begins to feel the emptiness of their achievement, seeing only 'doubtful joy'. She appears increasingly isolated and drained of energy as Macbeth moves away from her into his own troubled thoughts. She becomes more of an audience to Macbeth's words, rather than his partner. Although she rallies at the disastrous banquet, she ends that scene displaying none of her earlier dominance over her husband. Shakespeare does not show Lady Macbeth's decline into nervous breakdown and suicide, giving only one glimpse of that horrifying process: the torment she experiences in her sleepwalking.

In *Throne of Blood*, the Japanese film adaptation of *Macbeth*, Lady Macbeth stares at her hands in horror, aware of the evil she has unleashed.

Activities on characters

a You can build up your impression of a character by what they say, what other characters say about them, and by their actions. Follow Macbeth or Lady Macbeth through the play (you can use a similar method for any other character) and:

  • select lines or phrases they speak which you think are typical of him or her at particular moments;
  • collect examples of what is said by other characters about Macbeth or Lady Macbeth;
  • collect examples of Macbeth's or Lady Macbeth's actions (actions, as well as words, reveal what a character is like).

Either rehearse and present a short play, using all three types of example above.

Or make a visual display (for example a wall chart or a coursework folder of illustrations, quotations and your own comments).

Or use the three types of example to help you write an extended essay which analyses the character's journey through the play.

b Explore a character's motives in one of the following ways:

Hot-seating   One person steps into role as the character. Group members ask questions of the 'Why did you do this?' type.

Psychiatrist's couch   One person becomes the character and is psychoanalysed by a partner or small group.

Chat show   Your character appears as a celebrity on a television talk show and is questioned by the host.

Autobiography   Imagine yourself as a character. Write your life story.

Biography   Step into role as a character and write a biography of another character. For example, how would Malcolm write about Macbeth?

Chatroom   Each person in the group takes on the role of a character. Then enter a website chatroom and get discussion going!

Court of law   Take parts as judge, prosecution lawyers and defence lawyers to try Macbeth. The charge is that Macbeth is a usurper and tyrant who terrorised Scotland. You can call as witnesses other students taking roles as characters in the play (don't forget the Witches!).

Witches and witchcraft

Throughout Shakespeare's life, witches and witchcraft were the objects of morbid and fevered fascination. A veritable witch-mania characterised the reign of Elizabeth I, and many people suspected of being witches were cruelly persecuted. Those who were convicted faced the prospect of being burned to death.

Although some voices were raised against this superstitious and barbarous persecution, most people probably believed in witches. Hundreds of pamphlets describing the lurid details of many witchcraft trials were printed. They enjoyed enormous sales: the equivalent of today's popular newspapers, or films and books about the supernatural.

Witches were credited with diabolical powers. For example, they could predict the future, fly, sail in sieves, bring on night in daytime, cause fogs and tempests, and kill animals. They cursed enemies with fatal wasting diseases, induced nightmares and sterility, and could take demonic possession of anyone. Witches were able to raise evil spirits by concocting a horrible brew with nauseating ingredients.

It was believed that witches allowed the Devil to suck their blood in exchange for a 'familiar': a bird, reptile or beast as an evil servant. Accused witches were examined for the 'Devil's mark': a red mark on their body from which Satan had sucked blood (some of Shakespeare's audience might interpret Lady Macbeth's 'damned spot' as evidence of the Devil's mark).

Queen Elizabeth died in 1603 and was succeeded by King James. Under his rule, the morbid interest in witches continued. In 1604 an Act of Parliament decreed that anyone found guilty of witchcraft should be executed. Old women who lived alone and who kept cats were in danger of torture and death if they were accused of witchcraft.

This cruel persecution was fuelled by an ugly mixture of superstition, misogyny (hatred of women) and a firm conviction that religion and morality were being upheld. Those who confessed to being witches did so under torture or because they were in the grip of delusions that are today recognised as some form of mental illness.

◆ Paragraphs 3 and 4 above list many of the beliefs about witches held by Shakespeare's contemporaries. Identify in the script as many examples as you can of those beliefs.

King James was as fascinated by witchcraft as any of his subjects. In 1590 a group of witches tried to kill him. Their plot was discovered and they were brought to trial at North Berwick. The claims of one witch, Agnes Sampson, were sensational. She had collected toad venom to poison the king, christened a cat, tied parts of a dead man's body to it, sailed out to sea in a sieve and thrown cat and body-bits overboard to raise a storm to sink the king's ship.

King James personally interrogated one of the accused witches, Dr Fian. The poor doctor was horribly tortured: 'His nails upon all his fingers were riven and pulled off . . . his legs were crushed and beaten together as small as might be, and the bones and flesh so bruised that the blood and marrow spouted forth in great abundance'.

Fired by his experience of the trial, King James personally investigated other witchcraft cases. In 1597 he published *Demonologie*, a book on witchcraft. When he became King of England in 1603 he ordered its immediate printing in London.

In King James's England, although deep divisions existed between Protestants and Catholics, nearly everyone believed literally in heaven and hell, and lived in fear of eternal damnation: a consequence of witchcraft. Many of those watching *Macbeth* saw in the play the signs of a man and woman seized by demonic possession:

Trance 'Look how our partner's rapt' (page 17, line 141)

Changed appearance 'Why do you make such faces?' (page 85, line 67)

Inability to pray '"Amen" / Stuck in my throat' (page 45, lines 35–6)

Visions 'Is this a dagger which I see before me?' (page 41, line 33)

Disturbed behaviour 'I have a strange infirmity' (page 85, line 86)

Lack of fear 'I have almost forgot the taste of fears' (page 145, line 9)

Indifference to life 'She should have died hereafter' (page 147, line 16)

Invitations to evil spirits to possess one's body 'Come, you spirits' (page 25, line 38)

◆ Look through the illustrations showing the Witches. Reread the 'Witch' scenes (Act 1 Scenes 1 and 3, Act 3 Scene 5 and Act 4 Scene 1). Then write a new scene to follow the play's end. In it, the Witches meet to plan further mischief in Scotland.

The language of *Macbeth*

1 Imagery

Macbeth is rich in imagery: vivid words and phrases which conjure up emotionally charged mental pictures or associations. Imagery stirs the imagination, deepens dramatic impact, and gives insight into character. Certain images recur through the play, helping to create its distinctive atmosphere, perhaps most notably in the frequent images of blood (Macbeth imagines himself wading through a river of blood; Lady Macbeth, sleepwalking, tries to rub away the spot of blood; the 'blood-boltered Banquo' and so on).

Other recurring images include:

darkness (creating a pervasive sense of evil, as in Lady Macbeth's invocation, 'Come, thick night . . .');

clothes (Macbeth's usurpation of the throne dresses him in 'borrowed robes', illustrating the theme of deceptive appearance);

disease (the Witches' 'fog and filthy air' begins the imagery of sickness, which affects both Scotland, 'the sickly weal', and the Macbeths – she has a 'mind diseased', his mind is 'full of scorpions');

nature (frequent images of animals, birds and insects are often ominous, as in the cauldron scene).

◆ Choose one of the above images and collect as many examples as you can. Find an appropriate way of displaying your quotations.

All Shakespeare's imagery uses metaphor, simile or personification. All are comparisons.

A simile compares one thing to another using 'like' or 'as'. Macbeth challenges Banquo's Ghost to approach 'like the rugged Russian bear'; the First Witch threatens the sailor she will 'drain him dry as hay'.

A metaphor is also a comparison, suggesting that two dissimilar things are actually the same. Macbeth, hearing of the death of his wife, broods on life, seeing it as 'but a walking shadow, a poor player / That struts and frets his hour upon the stage / And then is heard no more'.

Personification turns all kinds of things into persons, giving them human feelings or attributes. The bleeding Captain speaks of Macbeth as 'Valour's minion' (bravery's favourite) and of 'Fortune' smiling on the rebel Macdonald.

Sometimes an image extends over several lines. For example in Act 1 Scene 7, lines 25–28, Macbeth soliloquises about whether or not to kill King Duncan, and concludes with an image from horse-riding:

> I have no spur
> To prick the sides of my intent, but only
> Vaulting ambition which o'erleaps itself
> And falls on th'other –

In this extended image of rider and horse, Macbeth sees himself like a horseman who urges on his mount by digging his spurs into the horse's sides. But he has no such motivation ('spur') to kill Duncan other than 'Vaulting ambition': like a rider vaulting onto his horse, but misjudging his leap in his over-enthusiasm and collapsing in failure on the other side.

Macbeth frequently uses strikingly visual images. After the disastrous appearance of Banquo's Ghost at the banquet, and knowing that Macduff has turned against him, he resolves to commit yet more murders. 'I am in blood / Stepped in so far that should I wade no more, / Returning were as tedious as go o'er' (Act 3 Scene 4, lines 136–8). He sees himself wading through a river of blood and is so far in that it does not matter whether he goes on or turns back.

♦ Use the information on these two pages to write an essay on what the imagery in *Macbeth* tells you about the atmosphere of the play and the character of Macbeth.

2 Antithesis

Antithesis is the opposition of ideas, words or phrases against each other, as in 'When the battle's lost, and won', 'Fair is foul, and foul is fair'. Antithesis expresses conflict ('lost' against 'won', 'fair' against 'foul') and is especially powerful in *Macbeth*, where good is set against evil, character against character, and where deception and false appearance are major themes. You will find antitheses everywhere in the play, but the Porter scene and Macbeth's 'If it were done . . .' (Act 1 Scene 7, lines 1–28) are particularly rich.

♦ Choose a scene or speech and identify the antitheses. As you speak the language, find physical ways to show the contrasts (for example by 'weighing' them with your hands or pushing and pulling arms with a partner).

3 Lists

Shakespeare enjoyed piling up words and phrases rather like a list. For example the Witches' gruesome ingredients for their cauldron are like a grotesque recipe (Act 4 Scene 1, lines 4–38). The Porter creates comedy as he lists the people going to hell (Act 2 Scene 3, lines 1–12). In Act 4 Scene 3, lines 57–60, Malcolm lists Macbeth's vices as the qualities of a bad king ('bloody, luxurious, avaricious . . .'), then goes on, in Act 4 Scene 3, lines 91–5, to list the dozen qualities of a good king ('justice, verity, temp'rance . . .'). Macbeth, talking with the Murderers, lists types of dog (Act 3 Scene 1, lines 92–6).

♦ Shakespeare's lists can be long or as short as three items ('In thunder, lightning, or in rain'). Select a list from the play that you enjoy and work out a way of acting each item (see, for example, page 118 Activity 1).

4 Creating new words

Shakespeare had the gift of making up new words. One method he used was to join words up with a hyphen. *Macbeth* is full of such hyphenated words, some so familiar that we do not recognise them as Shakespeare's creation (new-born, firm-set, new-hatched, live-long, bare-faced, cut-throat, earth-bound, lily-livered, bear-like).

♦ Search through the play for hyphenated words. Then write a story using as many of those words as possible. You may wish to add your own new words, created by using the hyphen.

5 Soliloquies

A soliloquy is a monologue, a kind of internal debate spoken by a character who is alone (or assumes he or she is alone) on stage. It gives the audience direct access to the character's mind, revealing their inner thoughts and motives. Macbeth often 'thinks aloud' (sometimes as an Aside), expressing doubt, fear, guilt, confusion and despair. For example his 'Tomorrow' soliloquy in Act 5 Scene 5 conveys his overwhelming despair. In Act 1 Scene 5, Lady Macbeth makes an impassioned appeal for demonic spirits to possess her.

◆ Identify each of the play's soliloquies. Choose one and write notes on how you would speak it on stage to maximise dramatic effect.

6 Verse and prose

Shakespeare's audiences expected tragedies to be written in verse, because verse was thought to be appropriate to great men, affairs of state, and moments of emotional or dramatic intensity. *Macbeth* is written mainly in blank verse: unrhymed lines with a five-beat rhythm (iambic pentameter). Each line has five iambs (feet), each with an unstressed ($\times$) and stressed ($/$) syllable:

$$\times \quad / \quad \times \quad / \quad \times \quad / \quad \times \quad / \quad \times \quad /$$

So foul and fair a day I have not seen.

In *Macbeth*, Shakespeare uses blank verse very flexibly. The five-beat rhythm is present, but less emphatically than in his earlier plays.

The Witches almost always speak in four-beat rhythm (tetrameter), a style appropriate to spells, incantations and the supernatural:

$$/ \quad\quad / \quad\quad\quad / \quad\quad /$$

Fair is foul, and foul is fair

Prose was conventionally used by low-status characters (the Porter, the Murderers), by characters in a state of madness (Lady Macbeth when sleepwalking), for comedy (the Porter, Lady Macduff's conversation with her son), and in letters (Macbeth's letter to his wife). Otherwise, in tragedy, high-status characters used verse. But Shakespeare often bends the rules: talking to the Murderers, Macbeth begins in prose, and later the Murderers use some verse.

◆ Choose a verse speech. Speak it emphasising the metre (4 or 5 beats). Then write eight or more lines of your own in the same style.

Macbeth in performance

The story goes that *Macbeth* was first performed before King James I at Hampton Court in 1606. No one knows for certain if that is true. The first record of a production was written by Simon Forman, who described a performance he saw at the Globe Theatre on Bankside in 1611. He summarises much of the plot, but claims to have seen Macbeth and Banquo on horseback. Perhaps he was thinking of a picture in Holinshed's *Chronicles* (see page 162), and had only heard the sound of horses' hooves. The actors probably added other sound effects: the whining, croaking and mewing of the Witches' familiars; thunder; the owl's screech; the clanging of the bell.

Since Shakespeare's time, *Macbeth* has always been popular. The diarist Samuel Pepys saw it at least three times in the 1660s and thought it excellent. But like all of Shakespeare's plays, *Macbeth* has been rewritten, revised and adapted through the centuries, reflecting the tastes and the social and political circumstances of different times.

Sir William Davenant (who claimed to be Shakespeare's illegitimate son) presented a radically changed version from that first published in the 1623 First Folio edition of all Shakespeare's plays. A record of his 1672 production reads:

> *The Tragedy of Macbeth*, altered by Sir William Davenant; being dressed in all its finery, as new clothes, new scenes, machines, as flyings for the witches; with all the singing and dancing . . . being all excellently performed being in the nature of an opera.

Macbeth became something of a musical spectacular with the Witches flying, dancing and singing in ever-increasing numbers. One nineteenth-century production put over a hundred witches on stage! There was little hesitation about cutting, amending or adding to the 1623 Folio version. Davenant cut the Porter and the Doctors, had Seyton change sides at the end, and altered the language so as not to offend his audience of gentry. Scenes were added: Lady Macbeth and Lady Macduff talked together. Macduff's role was greatly enlarged at the expense of Malcolm's. The Witches turned up to support Macduff against Macbeth.

Although there were attempts to return to the 1623 Folio script, the operatic additions to *Macbeth* persisted. Even those who wished to return to Shakespeare's version could not resist the temptation to make alterations. The great eighteenth-century actor David Garrick wrote a long dying speech for Macbeth, expressing sorrow and self-condemnation. Nineteenth-century productions depicted medieval Scotland in what were thought to be authentic sets and costumes. The onstage castles in *Macbeth* matched the Gothic mansions that the newly rich industrialists were building in the Scottish Highlands.

From early in the twentieth century the spectacular operatic effects were removed. Stagings became simpler, partly in an attempt to return to the plainer values of Shakespeare's own stage. Today most productions are based on the 1623 Folio script. But adaptation still takes place, and the play has been set in a Caribbean 'voodoo' culture, a hippy commune, Hitler's Germany, and the Great War of 1914–18.

Perhaps the best-known version of 'simple staging' is Trevor Nunn's 1976 Royal Shakespeare Company production (available on video). A small cast, working in a bare space defined by a chalk circle, created a memorably imaginative *Macbeth*. The play was set in what resembled a rehearsal studio rather than a traditional theatre. Actors sat on packing cases around the chalk circle, waiting for their moment

Macbeth is played and enjoyed all around the world. Select a line from the play as a suitable caption for this moment from a Japanese production.

to perform. There were no magical effects, but the production developed a powerful sense of mysterious evil.

The Witches have always presented directors with special problems and opportunities. Some directors make them virtually invisible, suggesting they exist as figments of Macbeth's imagination. Others present them as refugees or battlefield scavengers, existing in a bleak, militaristic world. They have been played as young and attractive women. One production presented them as a troupe of players, adopting various disguises and roles. Another had them as the Marx Brothers, manically stage-managing the entire play!

The relationship of Macbeth and his wife is fundamental to the play. Macbeth has wide-ranging relationships with almost all the other characters, but Lady Macbeth relates only to her husband. Actors have to decide how to play their relationship as they grow estranged from each other. A crucial aspect is how much they are in love, and some productions have presented their initial relationship as passionate and sensual. One famous remark about the production which starred Laurence Olivier and Vivien Leigh as the Macbeths was to remind audiences 'that Macbeth and his Lady were lovers before they were criminals'.

'You lack the season of all natures, sleep.' These are the last words Lady Macbeth speaks to her husband. He sits exhausted after the disastrous banquet at which he saw Banquo's Ghost. Step into role as Lady Macbeth and write an account of your feelings towards Macbeth from the moment you received his letter in Act 1 Scene 5 to the end of the banquet.

Shakespeare does not include a scene showing the coronation of Macbeth. In this production of Verdi's opera *Macbeth*, Lady Macbeth places the crown on Macbeth's head.

Macbeth at the Globe

The rebuilt Globe Theatre on London's Bankside staged a modern-dress production of *Macbeth* in 2001. Here, a terrified Macbeth reacts to Banquo's Ghost at the banquet.

The Witches in the Globe's modern-dress production.

Although spectacular productions are now rare, they can be immensely successful. An all-black adaptation of the play, *Umabatha*, has toured the world, appearing at the Globe Theatre in 2001. It transforms *Macbeth* into a play about Zulu identity in early nineteenth-century South Africa. Chanting, drumming, and rhythmically beating shields, a huge cast created a tribal *Macbeth* of immense ritual power. The Zulu warriors grieved, rejoiced, welcomed and fought throughout their own unique re-staging of Shakespeare's tragedy.

Stage your own production of *Macbeth*

Give reasons for the period and place in which you will set your production. In medieval Scotland? A modern office? A fascist state? Then choose several of the following activities to present as coursework.

◆ Design the set – how can it be used for particular scenes?
◆ Design the costumes – look at examples in this edition.
◆ Design the publicity poster – make a dazzling impact!
◆ Design the programme – content? illustrations? layout?
◆ Write character notes for actors' guidance.
◆ Work out a five-minute presentation to show potential sponsors.
◆ Design a website that gives details of your production.
◆ Video one scene or episode that will demonstrate how you will present one or more of the characters.

William Shakespeare
1564–1616

1564 Born Stratford-upon-Avon, eldest son of John and Mary Shakespeare.

1582 Marries Anne Hathaway of Shottery, near Stratford.

1583 Daughter, Susanna, born.

1585 Twins, son and daughter, Hamnet and Judith, born.

1592 First mention of Shakespeare in London. Robert Greene, another playwright, described Shakespeare as 'an upstart crow beautified with our feathers . . .'. Greene seems to have been jealous of Shakespeare. He mocked Shakespeare's name, calling him 'the only Shake-scene in a country' (presumably because Shakespeare was writing successful plays).

1595 A shareholder in The Lord Chamberlain's Men, an acting company that became extremely popular.

1596 Son Hamnet dies, aged eleven.
Father, John, granted arms (acknowledged as a gentleman).

1597 Buys New Place, the grandest house in Stratford.

1598 Acts in Ben Jonson's *Every Man in His Humour*.

1599 Globe Theatre opens on Bankside. Performances in the open air.

1601 Father, John, dies.

1603 James I grants Shakespeare's company a royal patent: The Lord Chamberlain's Men become The King's Men and play about twelve performances each year at court.

1607 Daughter, Susanna, marries Dr John Hall.

1608 Mother, Mary, dies.

1609 The King's Men begin performing indoors at Blackfriars Theatre.

1610 Probably returns from London to live in Stratford.

1616 Daughter, Judith, marries Thomas Quiney.
Dies. Buried in Holy Trinity Church, Stratford-upon-Avon.

The plays and poems
(no one knows exactly when he wrote each play)

1589–95 *The Two Gentlemen of Verona, The Taming of the Shrew, First, Second and Third Parts of King Henry VI, Titus Andronicus, King Richard III, The Comedy of Errors, Love's Labour's Lost, A Midsummer Night's Dream, Romeo and Juliet, King Richard II* (and the long poems *Venus and Adonis* and *The Rape of Lucrece*).

1596–9 *King John, The Merchant of Venice, First and Second Parts of King Henry IV, The Merry Wives of Windsor, Much Ado About Nothing, King Henry V, Julius Caesar* (and probably the *Sonnets*).

1600–5 *As You Like It, Hamlet, Twelfth Night, Troilus and Cressida, Measure for Measure, Othello, All's Well That Ends Well, Timon of Athens, King Lear.*

1606–11 *Macbeth, Antony and Cleopatra, Pericles, Coriolanus, The Winter's Tale, Cymbeline, The Tempest.*

1613 *King Henry VIII, The Two Noble Kinsmen* (both probably with John Fletcher).

1623 Shakespeare's plays published as a collection (now called the First Folio).